The Workhouse Donkey

The Workhouse Donkey was first produced on July 8, 1963, at the Chichester Festival Theatre. It concerns the cleaning up of a northern town by a new chief constable, who falls foul of the local Conservative Party, led by a titled brewer, and the local Labour Party, led by an ex-Mayor who is the 'Workhouse Donkey' of the play.

'The most successful play in the Brechtian style since Brecht wrote *The Caucasian Chalk Circle*.'

Martin Esslin

The Workhouse Donkey

A VULGAR MELO-DRAMA

BY

JOHN ARDEN

EYRE METHUEN LTD

The music for this play, by John Addison,
is available upon application to the
composer's agents:
London Management,
8 Upper Brook Street,
London, W1.

First published 1964
Reprinted 1966
Paperback edition 1966
Reprinted 1971
Reprinted 1974
by Eyre Methuen Ltd
11 New Fetter Lane
London EC4P 4EE
© *1964 by John Arden*
All rights reserved
Printed in Great Britain by
Whitstable Litho, Straker Brothers Ltd
ISBN 0 413 33070 2

FOR TAMARA

This cool sweet moon (now defeated by night
    Which crossed her with raincloud and mirk)
Had, under her first rising, sent momentary light
    Through every tree in the park.
Every bush, every pool, every thicket abhorrent
Remain to my blind sight apparent:
    And I can walk yet without danger or fright.

Author's Preface

I have called this play a melo-drama: a term I intend to be understood in its original sense of a play with a musical accompaniment. In the Chichester production, Mr Addison's score provided not only settings for the several songs but also a background for much of the dialogue, and linking passages between the scenes. The band was seated on an upper balcony of the stage and remained in view of the audience throughout the action. As the play is strictly a play and not a musical or a light opera, I dare say it would be possible to present it without instrumental accompaniment, but unless economy imperatively demands it, I do not recommend that this should be done.

The Workhouse Donkey was originally commissioned for the Royal Court Theatre, and it was necessary to adapt it somewhat for the open stage at Chichester. The directions in this printed text will, it is hoped, prove applicable to any of the more usual types of auditorium. For productions within a proscenium-arch it is essential that décor be kept to a minimum and that the action be allowed to flow from one scene into the next with the least possible delay. Both costumes and settings may have a certain air of caricature: but as the play is basically accurate and realistic (indeed, a great deal of it is conscientiously historical), the limits of visual extravagance normally adhered to by the artists of seaside picture-postcards should not be exceeded.

I had considerable difficulty in preparing *The Workhouse Donkey* for the stage. My chosen subject-matter proved both labyrinthine and intractable, and I do not think I could ever have condensed it into the bounds of conventional acting time without the assistance, advice, collaboration, criticism, and frequently expressed bewilderment of:

Mr Lindsay Anderson
Mr Stuart Burge
Miss Margaretta D'Arcy
Mr George Devine
Sir Laurence Olivier
and nearly everyone employed upon or connected with the
production at Chichester.

I am, however, still uncertain how valuable our combined
efforts have been. Two-and-a-half or three hours is normally
regarded as the maximum permissible length for a new play,
and under the conditions at present prevalent in our theatres it
is not easy to dispute this. But I would have been happy had it
been possible for *The Workhouse Donkey* to have lasted, say, six
or seven or thirteen hours (excluding intervals), and for the
audience to come and go throughout the performance, assisted
perhaps by a printed synopsis of the play from which they
could deduce those scenes or episodes which would interest
them particularly, and those which they could afford to miss.
A theatre presenting such an entertainment would, of course,
need to offer rival attractions as well, and would in fact take on
some of the characteristics of a fairground or amusement park;
with restaurants, bars, sideshows, bandstands and so forth, all
grouped round a central playhouse. The design of the playhouse itself would need careful consideration, as clearly members of an audience continually moving to and from their seats
in a conventional building will cause intolerable distraction.
But I am convinced that if what we laughably call 'vital theatre'
is ever to live up to its name, some such casual or 'prom-
concert' conception must eventually be arrived at.* It will not
suit every play, and every play should not be compelled to suit
itself to it: the theatre must be catholic. But it never will be

---

* Miss Joan Littlewood has already put forward a similar and
apparently highly practicable proposition. I hope she will be enabled
to carry it out.

catholic if we do not grant pride of place to the old essential
attributes of Dionysus:

> noise
> disorder
> drunkenness
> lasciviousness
> nudity
> generosity
> corruption
> fertility
>   and
> ease.

The Comic Theatre was formed expressly to celebrate them:
and whenever they have been forgotten our art has betrayed
itself and our generally accessible and agreeable god has hidden
his face.

The personality of the late Mr Joseph D'Arcy of Dublin
inspired much of the play.

The personality of my native town of Barnsley also inspired a
great deal of it: but I have carefully avoided the imitation of the
personalities of individual inhabitants. Thus the curiosity of
the malicious will go ungratified.

In view of the fact that this play was first performed in a
southern county, the speeches used as prologue and epilogue
were directed towards the probable audience in such a place.
In productions north of the Trent these speeches should be
replaced by those given on pages 135 and 136.

Some Critics said:
This Arden baffles us and makes us mad:
His play's uncouth, confused, lax, muddled, bad.

Said Arden:
Why do you accuse me and abuse me
And your polite society refuse me,
Merely because I wear no belt nor braces?
There would be reason for the wry mouths in your faces
And reason for your uncommitted halting speeches
If you would but admit I wore no bloody breeches.

JOHN ARDEN

The Workhouse Donkey

The Workhouse Donkey was first performed at the Chichester Festival Theatre on 8 July 1963, with the following cast:

Labour

ALDERMAN BOOCOCK, the Mayor	Dudley Foster
MRS BOOCOCK, the Mayoress	Fay Compton
ALDERMAN BUTTERTHWAITE, his friend and Ex-Mayor	Frank Finlay
HOPEFAST ⎫	Peter Russell
HARDNUTT ⎬ Borough Councillors	Harry Lomax
HICKLETON ⎭	Peter O'Shaughnessy

Conservative

ALDERMAN SIR HAROLD SWEETMAN, a wealthy brewer	Martin Boddey
LADY SWEETMAN, his wife	Alison Leggatt
MAURICE SWEETMAN, his son	Jeremy Brett
F.J., his friend: Industrialist and Borough Councillor	Peter Cellier

The Police

COLONEL FENG, Chief Constable	Anthony Nicholls
SUPERINTENDENT WIPER	Robert Stephens
SERGEANT LUMBER	Robert Lang
PC LIVERSEDGE	Derek Jacobi
PC LEFTWICH, retired from active duty: Mayoral Mace-Bearer and Town Hall Factotum	Keith Marsh
TWO POLICEMEN	Terence Knapp
	Raymond Clarke

The Electorate

DR WELLINGTON BLOMAX, a physician	Norman Rossington
WELLESLEY, his daughter	Mary Miller

GLORIA, Manageress of the Copacabana Club   Marion Mathie
STONE MASONS   Michael Turner
                                                  Michael Rothwell
GUESTS, at the Sweetmans'   Raymond Clarke,
Rowena Cooper, Marika Mann,
Jean Rogers
MAID, at the Sweetmans'   Louise Purnell
LANDLORD, of the Victoria and Albert   Dan Meaden
BARMAID   Elizabeth Burger
ASSISTANT BAR BOY   John Rogers
DRINKERS   Reginald Green, Terence Knapp,
Michael Rothwell, Michael Turner
NURSE, at Dr Blomax's   Rowena Cooper
DOORMAN   ⎤   Terence Knapp
HOSTESS   Irene Sutcliffe
WAITRESSES   at the   Rowena Cooper,
             Copacabana Club   Marika Mann
DANCERS   Elizabeth Burger, Rowena Cooper,
Jeanne Hepple, Louise Purnell,
Jean Rogers, Michael Rothwell
SPECIALITY   Jeanette Landis
  NUMBERS   ⎦
JOURNALISTS   Richard Hampton,
Michael Rothwell, Michael Turner
PARK ATTENDANT   Reginald Green
LOVERS   John Rogers, Louise Purnell
WAITRESS, in a Tea Shop   Jeanne Hepple
DEMONSTRATORS   Elizabeth Burger,
Reginald Green, Jeanne Hepple,
Jeanette Landis, Michael Rothwell

Produced by Stuart Burge
Music by John Addison
Décor by Roger Furse
Lighting by Richard Pilbrow
Dances arranged by Eleanor Fazan

The action of the play takes place in a Yorkshire industrial
town: somewhere between Sheffield and Leeds.
The time is the present.

Act One

A building site.
Foundation stone ready in position for lowering.

    Enter BLOMAX.

BLOMAX.
    Ladies and gentlemen: let us suppose we go
    From St Pancras to Sheffield,
    To Doncaster from King's Cross:
    By either route to Leeds.

    Enter MASONS

    Not very far to go, for us or the flight of a crow
    But involving geographically an appreciable mutation,
    (I mean, in landscape, climate, odours, voices, food.)
    I put it to you that such a journey needs
    In the realm of morality an equal alteration.

    Enter WIPER, LUMBER *and* PCs *as Guard of Honour.*

    I mean, is there anything you really believe to be bad?
    If you come to the North you might well think it good.
    You might well think, as I do,
    That you should change the shape of your faces
    Or even double their number
    When you travel between two places.

    Enter civic procession. It includes BOOCOCK, MRS BOO-
    COCK (LEFTWICH *with mace preceding them*), SWEET-
    MAN, F. J., *Labour Councillors, and* BUTTERTHWAITE.
    Aldermen and Mayor in robes of office, etc. Also Conserva-
    tive Ladies and YOUNG SWEETMAN, *and several Citizens.*

The values of other people
Are not quite as you understand them.
I would not overpraise them,
I would not recommend them,
I am certainly not here to offer to condemn them.
From the beginning to the end
Each man is bound to act
According to his nature
And the nature of his land.
Their land is different from yours.
Why, it has its own music.

Band plays 'Ilkley Moor'. BLOMAX *greets* WIPER, *receives
a curt nod in reply, and withdraws; enter* WELLESLEY,
meets BLOMAX *and stands with him.* WIPER *salutes the*
MAYOR.

WIPER. Guard of honour present and ready for your inspection, Mr Mayor.

BOOCOCK. Good afternoon. Superintendent, it is my privilege
to present to you your new chief constable, Colonel Feng.
Colonel Feng, Superintendent Wiper, who has during the
interregnum been very ably conducting . . .

FENG. Good afternoon, Superintendent.

WIPER. Good afternoon, sir.

FENG. Shall we have a look at the Guard of Honour, Mr
Mayor ?

BOOCOCK. Right we are, sir. After you.

FENG. Superintendent . . .

*The band plays 'Ilkley Moor' while they inspect the Con-
stables.* BUTTERTHWAITE *detaches himself from the
official group and comes down to the Masons. He holds an
unlighted cigarette in an ivory holder.*

BUTTERTHWAITE. Eh, begod: the old blue marching bull.
Brass bound and bloody minded. What a way to greet a

lovely day. Have you got such a thing as a light, Jack?

IST MASON. Here you are, Alderman.

BUTTERTHWAITE. Alderman? You ought to know me better nor that, lad!

IST MASON. All right then, Charlie, no offence intended.

BUTTERTHWAITE. That's a bit more like.

He indicates his Alderman's robe.

We may be garnished up like the roast beef of old England, but we haven't quite forgotten all realities yet, I hope. Blimey, look at that! Left right, left right, one two three, and how long have you been in the force, my fine fellow? Jolly good. Jolly good, give that man three stripes! Eh, the police force: we can't do without 'em, but my God how we hate 'em!

The inspection is now over and the MAYOR *takes his place by the stone.*

Watch it: here we go!

BOOCOCK. Fellow townsmen, ladies and gentlemen, er, voters. This afternoon's little ceremony is, as you might say, a double one. Clapping as it were two birds wi't 'yah billet. Firstly, we are laying the foundation stone for our new police headquarters: and secondly, we are paying a very hearty welcome indeed to our new chief constable: Colonel Feng. Both of these innovations will no doubt impinge upon our way of life in manifold directions.

MRS BOOCOCK. Most of these, I hope, pleasant. But I also hope to some of us unpleasant. And justly so!

Laughter.

BOOCOCK. Colonel Feng comes to us by the unanimous choice of the Borough Watch Committee.

BUTTERTHWAITE (*aside*). *He* said that. *I* didn't. Why, I wasn't even there at the time.

BOOCOCK. I am happy to say that the Conservative Members of that Committee, under the respected leadership of Sir Harold Sweetman –

He and SWEETMAN *exchange bows.* BUTTERTHWAITE *grinds his teeth.*

– have concurred entirely with the opinions of us, the majority party. This being a benevolent augury, I will now request the Chief Constable to say a few words. Colonel Feng.

FENG. Mr Mayor, Madam Mayoress, Aldermen, Councillors, ladies and gentlemen. I am not, I confess, a Northern man by birth, nor yet by upbringing. I trust this will be forgiven me.

Laughter.

My last post as Chief Constable was in an extremely different locality, where the prevalence of violent crime was such that only the firmest of firm hands would serve to eliminate it. It has been eliminated. We live in an age of overthrown moral standards. The criminal today is coddled and cosseted by the fantastic jargon of mountebank psychiatry. Yet I ask you, ladies and gentlemen, do these sentimental social pundits ever pause to reflect upon the agony literally suffered night after night by the women of this country who watch their menfolk go out to earn their daily bread; and they wonder (yes they do): 'Will he come home safe and sound, unbroken and unmaimed?' With God's help, ladies and gentlemen, I will put their minds at rest. Thank you.

Applause. BUTTERTHWAITE *gives a long low private whistle.*

BOOCOCK. And thank *you*, Colonel Feng. There will be many a loud hear hear to that, I dare well say . . . Now then: the laying of the stone. Who better can we ask to carry this out

than the man whom I might justly call the most honoured of
our leading citizens; Chairman of the Regional Branch of the
Labour Party, Secretary of the Local Mineworkers' Union,
controlling spirit of one-hundred-and-one hard-working
committees: and perhaps above all, the man who has held
the office of Mayor of this borough not fewer than nine times
altogether, which is, I believe, a national record!

2ND MASON (*aside to* BUTTERTHWAITE). In other words, the
only man in town who really pumps the oil. Am I right,
Charlie?

BUTTERTHWAITE (*aside to him*). You are.

BOOCOCK. Ladies and gentlemen, Alderman Charlie Butterthwaite. Give him a big hand. Come on, Charlie, you've a
job o' work to do here.

CHEERS. Three times three for Charlie B. Hooray, 'ray,
'ray . . .

Band plays 'See the Conquering Hero'.

BOOCOCK. By gummy. I can tell you, when I'm set up here in
these – (*He indicates his robes.*) alongside of old Charlie, I can't
help the feeling like I'm under false colours. They've all but
got his name wrote on the tab at back!

Laughter.

BUTTERTHWAITE. There he is again, nicking my gags. I'll tell
Colonel Feng on you for petty larceny! . . . You know, if
anyone o' you had come up to me a few years ago and told
me that this afternoon I'd find meself all set to trowel the
mortar for a new house for t' coppers, why, I'd ha' sent him
off to t'looney-bin with a good boot up his rump! But it
circles, you know, it all circles round. And as far as this town
goes, *we're* t' masters now. It warn't so easy to credit that in
1897 when your old uncle Charlie first saw the light of day in
the lying-in ward of the Municipal Workhouse. And 1926 I
call to my memory as a year of some bitterness, too. I fancy

Sir Harold Sweetman bears those days in mind. He and his confederates. They beat us at the time. But we fought and fought again, and in the end we won. And that's the end o' that. All that's left atween us now, is a few small political differences – overweighed (at least off duty) by an abiding sense of gratitude for Sir Harold's present enterprise. The Brewery Industry! Why, think of us without it! We'd be a dehydrated nation. And the frogs and the jerries, they could sweep us up like sawdust! Right: now where's this bit o' bricklaying? I've not got me union card, but I dare say we can accommodate any question o' demarcation troubles. Mortar mixed all right, Jack, is it?

1ST MASON. Aye, it's mixed.

BUTTERTHWAITE. What's your consistency?

1ST MASON. Twelve parts fine crushed stone: three parts lime putty: one part Portland cement.

BUTTERTHWAITE. Not bad at all. I like to see good workmanship. Trowel? Right. Any young lass down there want the icing smoothed over her wedding cake? She's only to say the word. I'm ready and willing for t' usual consideration.

He smacks a kiss or two towards the audience.

Nobody? All right. Here we go . . . send it down, David.

The stone is lowered on to the mortar he has spread.

It gives me great pleasure to declare this stone well and truly laid. (*He taps the corners with his trowel.*) Knock, knock, knock and it's done. Any more for any more?

BOOCOCK (*restraining him*). Wait up, Charlie. Steady . . .

All stiffen as the band breaks into the National Anthem. Then the group begins to break up and converse in knots.

LUMBER. Guard of Honour, right turn. To your duties: quick march!

He marches out with the Constables. Citizens disperse.
WIPER *bumps into* BUTTERTHWAITE.

BUTTERTHWAITE. After you, Mr Wiper.
WIPER. After you, Mr Butterthwaite.
BUTTERTHWAITE. Alderman Butterthwaite, *if* you please.

LADY SWEETMAN *and* YOUNG SWEETMAN *enter and talk with* SWEETMAN. F. J., BLOMAX *and* WELLESLEY *also come back on stage, and* BUTTERTHWAITE *sees him.*

Hello, Wellington. Is that you? I think that wor one o' my better efforts. Don't you agree?
BLOMAX. Oh, very good. Very lively, Charlie.
BUTTERTHWAITE. I'll be there at ten sharp, at the usual table.

BUTTERTHWAITE *moves away towards his Labour Councillors.*

BLOMAX. As great Bonaparte wishes . . . What he meant to say was: that this evening at ten o'clock there will be an extraordinary meeting of the working caucus committee of the Labour Party at the east end of the saloon bar of the Victoria and Albert Hotel. Alderman Butterthwaite will be in the chair. And everybody else is to hang upon his words, as is usual: as is dutiful: as is after all only convenient. Does it appear to you strange a professional man like me should hail this clown as Bonaparte? The Napoleon of the North, as we matily describe him up here? Well, professional or not, I am a corrupted individual: for every emperor needs to have his dark occult councillor: if you like, his fixer, his manipulator – me. I do it because I enjoy it. I have also in my time enjoyed the delights of carnality – a less anti-social corruption perhaps, but in my case very often a swollen carbuncle of unexpected peril. You see, I am a doctor. My name is Wellington Blomax. I have not yet been struck off the register, but as you will find, it's been a pretty close thing.

(*He introduces* WELLESLEY *to the audience.*) Here I am confronted by the fruits of my loose studenthood. This poor girl without a mother is my own daughter: Wellesley. She came back home only a day or two ago after a sufficiently long absence. She works for her living and her education (I may say: at my expense) has been regrettably incompetent. Really, we hardly know each other.

WELLESLEY *gives a short laugh. So does he.*

But I conceive it my duty to introduce her at once to the local opportunities and make up for what she's missed.

BUTTERTHWAITE (*on the way out with Labour Councillors*). I think I've told everybody, but in case I missed one out, just confirm it, will you?

BLOMAX. I'll attend to it, Charlie.

Exit BUTTERTHWAITE, *etc.*

WELLESLEY. Would you say he was one of them?

BLOMAX. One of what?

WELLESLEY. The Local Opportunities.

BLOMAX. Oh, my dearie, no. He's on my National Health, but . . . no, no, no, what *you* want, my sweetheart, is the altogether opposite aspect of this deplorable townscape.

BLOMAX *points to* SWEETMAN.

Now the heavy gentleman over there . . .

WELLESLEY. Who's the young one with him?

BLOMAX. His son and heir, my sweetheart. Sweetman's Amalgamated Brewery and Corn Products – enormous – luxurious . . .

WELLESLEY. I've already met him, thank you very much. We shared a compartment on the way down from Penrith.

YOUNG SWEETMAN *sees her and comes over.*

YOUNG SWEETMAN. Hello there.

WELLESLEY. Hello.

He leads her away from her father.

YOUNG SWEETMAN. You know, I knew perfectly well we were going to see each other again within less than three days. Now this time you are most definitely going to tell me who you are and what you are doing here and what I have to do to get to know you better . . .

The CONSERVATIVES *group together with* FENG. WELLESLEY *in conversation with* YOUNG SWEETMAN. *A* MAID *brings in a tray of drinks and the group becomes a cocktail party.*

SCENE TWO

Sweetman's House. SWEETMAN, LADY SWEETMAN, YOUNG SWEETMAN, FENG, F. J., TWO LADIES, WELLESLEY, MAID; BLOMAX *still on stage in foreground.*

BLOMAX.
   Aha, does she not show a very pretty accomplishment ?
   A long-neglectful father need not scruple to hide
   The trickling down of a tear of pride ?

Exit BLOMAX.

SWEETMAN. Yes, Colonel Feng, what you saw and heard today is by no means unusual.

F. J. He does it all the time.

SWEETMAN. Yes. He was born in the workhouse: he conducted and ruined single-handed the General Strike: and he's everybody's Uncle Charlie and will remain so till he dies.

LADY SWEETMAN. Or until he's voted out. I'm quite sure it's not impossible. You talk about him all the time as though he were . . .

SWEETMAN. We are talking, my dear, about the man whose Napoleonic organization of the Socialist party machine . . .

F. J. Particularly in regard to the disposition of ward boundaries . . .

SWEETMAN. Yes, ward boundaries. It's all organized, you see. Overriding majority: organised by gerrymandering, and intended to continue. Such – Colonel Feng – is the lamentable framework into which, you will discover, you will have to accommodate yourself speedily, or else you will be . . .

1ST LADY. What do you think of it, Colonel Feng?

FENG. I have really no opinion, dear lady. I represent the force of law. I can have no opinion of political matters.

SWEETMAN. Yes. You will discover.

2ND LADY. Of course, the people do enjoy his speeches. You do have to laugh at them.

1ST LADY. Laugh at naughty children.

F. J. He rehearses it, of course.

LADY SWEETMAN. But, of course, we have to smack them.

WELLESLEY. Really have to smack? I mean, for providing entertainment? I mean, is the town really so badly misgoverned?

A pause.

YOUNG SWEETMAN. Misgoverned? Oh, it's not exactly misgoverned. It's just the wrong lot are the governors, that's all.

WELLESLEY. You see, if Colonel Feng says 'no politics' and yet he sees the town misgoverned, I mean really misgoverned . . . what do you do then, Colonel?

FENG. I rely, my dear young lady, upon the integrity of the British policeman. We live in an age of overthrown moral standards, and . . .

WELLESLEY. You said that at the ceremony.

FENG. So I did.

WELLESLEY. What about the moral standards of the British policeman? Are his overthrown as well?

LADY SWEETMAN. I suppose really the trouble is, we women, we see the personal side. While all the men all the time are looking for points of principle. But what I so dislike about people like Butterthwaite, they are not only so vulgar themselves but they expect everybody else to live at the same level. I don't see why I should. I cannot forgive them the way they deprived this town of our art gallery. It was a very nice little gallery, Colonel Feng – old masters, quite well spoken of. A genuine Titian, and there were 'Cows in a Field'. They gave it to Cuyp, but I believe it could be a Rembrandt. I have always been something of a connoisseur myself. In a small way, a collector. And so has Sir Harold.

SWEETMAN. Yes, moderns, mostly.

LADY SWEETMAN (to WELLESLEY). You must tell me all about yourself, my dear. My boy tells me he met you on a train . . .

SWEETMAN. Who is she?

YOUNG SWEETMAN. I met her the other day. Her father's a doctor.

SWEETMAN. And what does *she* do?

YOUNG SWEETMAN. She works in the forest.

SWEETMAN. Works in the what?

YOUNG SWEETMAN. The Forestry Commission. They plant trees in Westmorland.

SWEETMAN. A doctor, you said. Do I know him?

YOUNG SWEETMAN. I don't know. His name is Blomax.

SWEETMAN. Yes. He's a rogue and the crony of rogues. Did you ever meet her mother? She was as black as your hat.

YOUNG SWEETMAN. I don't believe you.

SWEETMAN. Yes. She was a Maltese. You will discover.

F. J. Is she one of that young crowd of yours at the Copacabana Club?

YOUNG SWEETMAN. Ha, ha. Oh no, not her.

SWEETMAN. The Copacabana? I didn't know you went there? Well, don't you go again. It's a sort of a dinner and dancing establishment, Colonel Feng. Nothing very horrifying.

F. J. Pretty tame compared to London.

SWEETMAN. Yes, and pretty trivial too . . . Of course, Colonel Feng, you might say all forms of pleasuring are pretty trivial when it comes down to it. All it usually comes down to in this town is the bottom of a pint pot—

YOUNG SWEETMAN. The bottom of half a dozen pint pots.

SWEETMAN. Half a dozen ? Two dozen. Three dozen. Four. Drink themselves sick.

F. J.
And not uncommonly after licensed hours.

SWEETMAN.
An instructive experiment that you might well try
To sound the ground for your new job, I mean . . .

F. J.
Why don't you – Colonel – send a man or two
To the Victoria and Albert at half past eleven ?

SWEETMAN.
Tonight perhaps.

F. J.
Tonight most suitable.

SWEETMAN.
Yes.

FENG.
A public house ?

SWEETMAN.
Hotel.

YOUNG SWEETMAN.
Not one
Of ours, of course. A free house. *We* don't go there.

FENG.
You wish to lay an information, do you,
Sir Harold ?

SWEETMAN.
No. Emphatically no.

We speak (in passing) of our town folks' pleasure
And – what was it she said – misgovernment?
Monopoly and party have controlled
This town for thirty years. Consider it
And consider, sir, the grave unlikelihood
That you can live and serve here and yet hold
Upon our politics no opinion, sir.

FENG.

I think, Sir Harold, I discern your working.

SWEETMAN.

Yes . . .

FENG.

Then I will tell you *mine*. I am here
To keep the law. And therefore must begin
By testing at all points the law you keep
Already, and how you keep it. Public houses
Are indeed one point. But only one. And who
Frequent such public houses, or such clubs,
Or hotels if you call them so, or what
Or where – is neither here nor there! Provided
That the law is kept. And where not kept
I should be glad of relevant information,
Or none at all. I do not know you, sir.
I do not know this people. And I must test
The whole community according to
The rigid statutes and the statutes only.
I can assure you now without vainglory
My testing will be thorough.

SWEETMAN.

Yes.

The MAID *whispers to* LADY SWEETMAN.

LADY SWEETMAN.

Dinner is served. Shall we go in?
Colonel?

FENG.

    Delighted, madam. After you.

YOUNG SWEETMAN (*to his father*).

    Are you quite sure he's ours?

SWEETMAN.

    What d'you mean?

    Go in to dinner . . . After you, F. J.

F. J.

    No, no, H. S. I follow after *you* . . .

      Exeunt.

SCENE THREE

Saloon bar of the Victoria and Albert.
    Enter BLOMAX *and several drinkers.*
    LANDLORD *behind his bar.*

BLOMAX. Big-hearted Arthur!

1ST DRINKER. No, no, no . . . Of course that horse is going to run . . .

2ND DRINKER. It's going to run at Beverley Races: there's no question about it . . .

3RD DRINKER. It was said very clearly . . .

BLOMAX. Big-hearted Arthur will be a non-starter! The information is confidential, but the oracle has delivered it. Alarm and despondency now spread like wildfire through celebrated Northern turf circles . . . Who's going to fill me?

4TH DRINKER (*handing him a glass*). Here you are, Doctor.

BLOMAX (*looking at him sharply*). Hello, hello, hello, I don't know you. You're not one o' my patients?

4TH DRINKER. Not exactly, no . . . but I dare say I *could* be?

1ST DRINKER. I dare say he *could* be. I'll vouch for him, Doctor.

BLOMAX (*clearing a space on a table, takes a pad of forms out*).

Very well then, so be it. Always carry me blank forms ready. You see . . . Name, address and previous medical adviser ?

4TH DRINKER *whispers in his ear.*

(*Writing.*) Now sign on the line, sir . . . Now then, what's the trouble ? And how can I cure it ? A little matter of a certificate perhaps ? Easily arranged . . .

4TH DRINKER *whispers again.*

Aha, you were down with a runny tummy, were you, so you couldn't possibly have been out burgling ? Couldn't you ? I wonder . . . No, it won't do. I steer very clear of courts of law, my dear sir. If it had to come up anywhere else, I would do your documents with pleasure . . . but . . .

4TH DRINKER *shoves some money over to him.*

All right, I will consider it. But I'm very very doubtful . . .

GLORIA *enters and comes up to* BLOMAX.

GLORIA. For the sake of old times, can we have a little word ?
BLOMAX. Gloria! Good gracious me! We don't expect to find you these days slumming it in the midst of the town in this dreary old boozing-ken! Gentlemen, you all know Gloria! – Get her a drink! – I am surprised, my dear Gloria, that you can tear yourself away from that expensive establishment of yours out there on the bypass . . . (*He addresses the audience.*) . . . known for your information as the Copacabana Club. And this most elegant and most gorgeous lady – who was for a space my very close friend – is now the manageress. There you are: You all know Gloria. What you don't know – I fancy – is where the money comes from that keeps that club going. *I* don't know it either.
GLORIA. *I'm* not going to tell you.
BLOMAX. What *are* you going to tell me ?
GLORIA. I want professional advice of a rather private nature.

Are you acquainted with Superintendent Wiper of our local police ?

BLOMAX. How d'you do, in public. Not much else beyond that.

GLORIA. This isn't for in public. Let's go to the back.

She moves upstage. BLOMAX *is about to follow her when* BUTTERTHWAITE, BOOCOCK *and* LABOUR COUNCILLORS *all come in.*

BLOMAX. Wait a moment, we're interrupted! The processional entrance. They need to have a tune! Charlie, Mr Mayor, how are you ? How are you ?

BUTTERTHWAITE. We need to have a tune. And some words to it and all. Dr Wellington, oblige.

BLOMAX (*sings*).
When Bonaparte assumed his crown
He put it on himself.
He was sole author of his power
And he piled his private wealth.
He kept his throne with sword and gun,
Dragoon and Cuirassier,
He marched with cannon at either flank
And bayonets in his rear.

BUTTERTHWAITE (*sings*).
But I am not the same as that:
I bow to the public voice.
My best endeavours are bent thereto
As befits the people's choice—

He sees BLOMAX *is going out after* GLORIA.

Hey, what about the rest of it ?

BLOMAX. You'll have to do it for yourself. I'm temporarily prevented. (*He joins* GLORIA.)

BUTTERTHWAITE (*shouting after him*). I wish you were temporarily prevented from one or two other activities.

BLOMAX returns and takes BUTTERTHWAITE aside.

BLOMAX. Which reminds me. Do you know what won the three-forty?

BUTTERTHWAITE. It did come to my ears. And I should like to know why, when you recommend a horse, it always develops spavins afore it reaches t'starting-gate. I gave you that money to put on for me on what you swore was a dead cert.

BLOMAX. Correction, Charlie. Twice. All you gave me was one of your promises: and as usual you chose to override my considered recommendation in favour of what you were told by some half-cock informant at the Miners' Union offices. I'm no bookie's runner, you know: but even if I was, I'd need to be paid for it.

BUTTERTHWAITE. You can't be paid today. Are you being pressed for t'cash?

BLOMAX. No, not exactly, but . . .

BUTTERTHWAITE. And what'd you expect me to do for you if you were? Burgle t'town hall?

BLOMAX. Why not? You're the great dictator, aren't you?

BUTTERTHWAITE. Get away with you, go on!

> *BLOMAX retires with* GLORIA. BUTTERTHWAITE *and party sit down round a table and the other drinkers move politely away from their vicinity. The* LANDLORD *brings their drinks.*

Barney, you have now seen the new Chief Constable. Both publicly ceremonious and privately confidential over the well-oiled social harmony of the Mayor's parlour. What do you think of him?

BOOCOCK. He's a change from t'last one, isn't he? He's got integrity; he's got energy; he's got a power of command. Of course, there won't be much for him to do.

BUTTERTHWAITE. That's just the trouble, ain't it?

HICKLETON. What do you mean?

BUTTERTHWAITE. A compendium of all the qualities Mr Mayor has just named, if he finds himself idle he looks for a job o' work. What I ask is: where?

BOOCOCK. I could indicate a few places. You remember what he said about overthrown moral standards? Now, you take that new club that's opened up on the bypass. The Coco . . . Capoco . . . the . . . er . . .

BUTTERTHWAITE. The Cocoa-banana?

BOOCOCK. Or whatever it might be. I believe it is described as a nightclub-cum-roadhouse. I'd call it an expense-account brothel.

HOPEFAST. There's no proof of that; is there?

BOOCOCK. There isn't. But in my opinion that licence should never have been issued without a few more searching questions. I've been hearing stories. There's dancing there, you know. And a great deal of it is in the nude.

BUTTERTHWAITE. Who's in the nude?

BOOCOCK. I've been hearing stories. It's come in from London, and it's not what we're used to.

HARDNUTT. Whose money's at back of it?

BOOCOCK. I don't know and I don't care. But young Sweetman and his debutantey riff-raff have been frequenting it pretty frequent. And you're not telling me *their* tastes are all in the nature of an advanced class in metallurgy at the technical college. I have already passed the word to Colonel Feng and I hope he takes a look.

BUTTERTHWAITE. Ah, we don't want to interfere with the pleasures of our gilded youth, Barney. They're an ornament to the town.

BOOCOCK. The late-night traffic accident reports are an ornament to the town and all – by – if I had my way I'd set some o' them gilded youth to a couple 'years down t'pit. But then I never do have my way. So what's the bloody odds?

GLORIA *moves towards the door*, BLOMAX *trotting behind her.*

GLORIA. All right then, I'm off. I'll waste no more time. If you won't do it, you won't.

BLOMAX. I didn't say I wouldn't.

HICKLETON (*watching her*). Oho, ho, ho!

BUTTERTHWAITE (*watching her*). Well now, I'm looking at a very privileged old divorcé indeed.

BLOMAX (*to* GLORIA). I said only what I always say. I'm promising nothing . . .

GLORIA *sweeps out.*

HICKLETON. You know who she is, don't you?

BUTTERTHWAITE. No. Who is she?

HICKLETON. What Barney wor just talking about. She runs the bloody place.

BUTTERTHWAITE. Oh! Dr Blomax, come here!

BLOMAX *obeys him.*

HICKLETON. We're all admiring your taste, lad. May we make so bold as to poke in our noses and ask . . .

BOOCOCK. We don't want to interfere, but . . .

BUTTERTHWAITE. But our attention has been drawn to what we might call the pursuits of your fair lady companion.

BOOCOCK. And I am sure you will agree with me, Doctor, that the immorality in this town has got to be very firmly checked.

BLOMAX. Mr Mayor, all I know of the lady is that she is a patient. She is under the seal of the oath of Hippocrates, which is not the same thing as the French word for hypocrites. I'm sorry, there it is.

BUTTERTHWAITE. Eh dear, we're getting ethical. We *do* stand rebuked. Come on, take a seat. Now, to return to business. We have been discussing the character of our latest public servant. And I regret to inform you our opinions are divided. When that appointment was made, I was flat on me back in the Municipal Hospital with me mortifying gallstones. But if I'd known they'd agreed on *him*, I'd ha' dragged meself up and come down on that Watch Committee and vetoed the whole bang shoot!

BOOCOCK. If you had, you'd ha' been a fool There is not a shadow of reason . . .

BUTTERTHWAITE (*thumping his belly*). I don't need reasons. I *know* it in here!

BLOMAX. I wouldn't go so far as to say you weren't right.

BUTTERTHWAITE. Why ? Have you heard summat ? Come on, what's Feng been up to ?

BLOMAX. Nothing very significant. But I *have* been given the word that tonight he is taking his dinner with His Majesty, Lord Sweetman. Her Ladyship in attendance very gracious over the braised lamb, and innumerable assistance provided by members of the entourage.

BOOCOCK. Well, what's so strange about that ? He's entitled to eat his dinners where he wants, I suppose ?

BUTTERTHWAITE. I wouldn't be too sure. A Chief Constable is maintained to be a non-political office. If the first thing he does when he comes into a town is to huddle over his grub with a pack of roaring Tories, I claim he wants watching. What you're going to find is an insidious partisan: And if that's the road it turns out, *I'm* not going to dry your eyes for you. Why couldn't you have invited him to dinner yersen ?

BOOCOCK. He's welcome any time to tek a sup o'tea wi' me and Mrs Boocock, but . . .

BUTTERTHWAITE. Oh Barney, Barney, Barney, you've no bloody notion, have you ? All right, but you'll discover, as somebody might put it . . . Any particular problems due up at t'next Council Sessions ?

LANDLORD. Last orders, everybody. Last orders, if you please.

BOOCOCK. I'm sorry to say that it's the same old perennial. The future of the art gallery.

BUTTERTHWAITE. Oh my gracious God.

BOOCOCK. Sweetman wants to make it an issue.

BUTTERTHWAITE. No, look, now look here! I'm sick to bloody death of that art gallery. In 1939 we took it over as an emergency annexe to the Municipal Hospital. There wor no opposition. Since then it's proved its necessity one hundred and ten per cent. Every single meeting of the Hospital Management Committee has confirmed the state of affairs. Dammit, the Chairman is my cousin's brother-in-law. I ought to know. And what about my gallstones? Wellington, bear testimony!

BLOMAX *nods agreement.*

BOOCOCK. Sweetman lays claim we could afford a new hospital and return the art gallery to its original function. What's more, he says he has some pictures of his own he wants to donate.

BUTTERTHWAITE. There is a regular diesel service on the hour every hour into Wakefield and Leeds, and good art galleries in both places. If people want pictures, let them go there. There is no demand for art in this town.

BOOCOCK. It could be an election issue.

BUTTERTHWAITE. Do you seriously imagine the ratepayers are going to stand to be plucked for a new bloody hospital? Godsake, have some common!

BOOCOCK. It ought to be considered, though.

BUTTERTHWAITE. Considered who by?

BOOCOCK. The Ways and Means Committee for a start. I've got it marked down for the agenda on Tuesday.

BUTTERTHWAITE. There's a pair o' Sweetman's pensioners w' seats on that Committee. They could use it to make trouble and hold up other business.

LANDLORD. Time, gentlemen, please.

BOOCOCK. I would like it attended to, Charlie.

BUTTERTHWAITE. All right. I'll attend to it.

LANDLORD (*putting some lights out*). Gennelmen, *if* you please. Closing time, gennelmen. Time if you please!

BOOCOCK. Right. Well, we'd best be off home. Are you coming along?

BUTTERTHWAITE. No. I've got a chap I want to see down the Pontefract Road. I'll see you tomorrow.

BOOCOCK. Goodnight to you, Charlie.

BUTTERTHWAITE. Night night, me old Barney . . .

DRINKERS (*going out*). Night, Mr Mayor . . . Night, Charlie. Night, Frank . . . (*etc.*)

The stage empties except for COUNCILLORS, BUTTER-THWAITE, LANDLORD *and* BLOMAX.

BUTTERTHWAITE. Let's have another round, Frank.

LANDLORD. Wait up a minute. I've got to draw me curtains . . .

BUTTERTHWAITE. Who's on the beat tonight? PC Liversedge?

LANDLORD. Should be by rights.

BUTTERTHWAITE. Grand. We're all clear then.

The drinks are brought as they resume their seats round the table.

Now look here, I'm not having it. If everybody in this Council was to dilly-dally around after Barney Boocock's formalities, nowt'd get done. Nowt. Who have we got here belonging to the Ways and Means? One, two, three. Right. There's enough for a quorum. Alderman Butterthwaite i't'chair, Councillors Hopefast, Hardnutt and Hickleton present in committee – er – Doctor Wellington Blomax, Deputy Secretary. I declare the Committee in session.

HOPEFAST. I move that the minutes of the previous meeting be taken as read.

HARDNUTT. Seconded.

BUTTERTHWAITE. Votes? All right. Passed. So the motion

before this Committee is that the time is not yet ripe for consideration of the reversal of the Municipal Hospital Annexe to its original function.

HICKLETON. Seconded.

BUTTERTHWAITE. Right. Anybody agen it? I should bloody well hope there's nobody agen it . . . All right. Very good. Motion passed, nem con. And our flash Harry Sweetman can wear that in the brim of his Anthony Eden and go to church with it . . .

Enter PC LIVERSEDGE.

LIVERSEDGE. Ha, h'm.

BUTTERTHWAITE. Evening, Liversedge. How are you? Have a pint of ale. It's on the Corporation.

LIVERSEDGE. Are you aware, sir, that it is after permitted hours?

HOPEFAST. Don't talk so daft.

LIVERSEDGE. You'll have to excuse me, Councillor. But I have my duty to perform.

BUTTERTHWAITE. You have your *what*? Look, lad. We're discussing local government business in here. You ought to be aware of that by now. What the hell d'you think you're playing at?

LIVERSEDGE. Alderman, I'm sorry, but it's very particular orders.

BUTTERTHWAITE. Orders. Whose orders?

LIVERSEDGE. There's been summat of a shake-up. You see, it . . .

Enter LUMBER *and another* PC.

LUMBER. Right, Liversedge. Who have you found? Oh! I might have guessed it.

HARDNUTT. Come on then, Sergeant. Where's the handcuffs?

LUMBER. Now, Councillor, you know it's not a matter for

handcuffs. But I *shall* have to ask you gentlemen for your names and addresses.

BUTTERTHWAITE. Oh for Godsake, flatfoot, go and get stuffed! If you don't know who we are, *I'm* not going to bloody tell you! I remember the days in 1926 I'd ha' took twelve o' you bluebottles on wi' nowt but me two boots and a twist o' barbed wire round me pick heft. What were *you* doing then?

LUMBER. When?

BUTTERTHWAITE. The General Strike 1926 I'm talking about! I know what you were doing. You warn't even wetting on your poor mother's apron. You wor nowt but a dirty thought atween your dad and his beer. . . . There's no question this is Feng! Wellington, go round to the station tomorrow and see that slimy Wiper. Find out what's happening and how serious it is. (*To the police.*) Get out o' my road.

BLOMAX (*to the police as he leaves*). Quis custodiot ipses custodias? Good night to the lot of you . . .

   Exeunt

SCENE FOUR

A street.
Enter WELLESLEY *and* YOUNG SWEETMAN.

WELLESLEY. Was I not dressed well enough to suit you?

YOUNG SWEETMAN. You were beautifully dressed.

WELLESLEY. But you say that to all the girls you bring home with you to dinner.

YOUNG SWEETMAN. I don't bring all the girls home.

WELLESLEY. Then why did you bring me? I would much rather you'd taken me out to an expensive restaurant or something.

YOUNG SWEETMAN. There *are* no expensive restaurants.

WELLESLEY. Yes, there are. In Leeds. And what about that club?

YOUNG SWEETMAN. The Copacabana? It's not really the sort of place . . .

WELLESLEY. It's very expensive.

YOUNG SWEETMAN. In any case I had to be at home this evening. Because of the Chief Constable and all the family prestige and so on. And I wasn't going to let you escape from me again like you did at the station. There's another thing, if we bring a girl home round here . . . it means that we want to . . .

WELLESLEY. To present her to the authorities as a future associate? You ought to have told me that before. You could even have proposed before. In a respectable formal fashion. Now it's too late. You tell me I didn't find favour. I wasn't dressed well enough.

YOUNG SWEETMAN. Wellesley, I have said you were beautifully dressed!

WELLESLEY. Describe me, if you please.

YOUNG SWEETMAN. Now, Wellesley, look here . . .

WELLESLEY. Go on, Maurice. Describe me. Let me hear if you still mean it.

> BLOMAX *enters. The other two do not notice him.*

YOUNG SWEETMAN.

> As I was lying on my bed
> And my eyelids blue with sleep
> I thought I saw my true love enter,
> Golden and dusty were her feet.
> Her gown of green, it let be seen
> Her shoulders white and brown,
> Her hair was tied in a high tight ribbon
> As sleek as a pool of trout
> And her earlobes like the Connemara Marble
> Moved quietly up and about.

WELLESLEY. As I breathed, I suppose?

YOUNG SWEETMAN. As you breathed, and as you were eating. I mean, that was the impression.

WELLESLEY. Then why can't I go there again?

YOUNG SWEETMAN. Oh, Wellesley, for God's sake . . . I have been trying to explain to you. You should have given me a different name. Your father – *you* ought to know it. For God's sake how could I? They don't tell me all the scandal. He is not persona grata, at my father's or anywhere else.

BLOMAX (*coming forward*). Indeed, and why not?

YOUNG SWEETMAN. Oh, we're overheard. I wasn't talking to you.

BLOMAX. You were talking *about* me. I may very well be a corrupted individual, but let me inform you I am a graduate of Edinburgh University, which is not to be squirted at, and I clap MD to the rear quarters of my name . . . with very high honours. What's the matter with that?

YOUNG SWEETMAN. To put it quite bluntly, sir: You don't have enough money. You're a resident of this town; you don't need me to tell you the sine qua non.

BLOMAX. Ho, the 'gracilis puer perfusus liquidis odoribus sub antro'! Don't you try and blind me with your hic haec hoc, young man! I've heard about *you* . . . and I'm not at all sure you're a fit companion for my beautiful daughter. (*He tries to put his arm round* WELLESLEY, *but she shrugs him off.*) To whom I have a manifest duty, she being in her origins an unfortunate mistake; as was also her dear mother, now – alas – divorced and forgotten, but traumatic in my history.

(*Sings.*)

> I married my wife because I had to
> Diddle di doo: Di doo doo-doo
> My wedding day in the month of May
> The honeymoon in flaming June
> A babe of shame of such ill fame

All it wants is an honest name
I married my wife because I had to
Diddle di doo : di doo doo-doo . . .

Now sir, be off . . . before I ask you your intentions.

YOUNG SWEETMAN. Oh my God . . . Wellesley . . . I . . .

WELLESLEY. I think you'd better go. You're only making things worse.

YOUNG SWEETMAN. All right. But it's not finished.

WELLESLEY. Isn't it ?

YOUNG SWEETMAN. No. I mean . . . no, it's not finished . . .

Exit YOUNG SWEETMAN.

WELLESLEY. Thank you very much. I'm sure it was well intended.

BLOMAX. All I am doing is to pursue my way of life. I put you on to him. It's up to you to hold him. If my reputation is a stumbling-block, I might very well remind you that half of that reputation is caused by what caused *you*. So why don't you go home and wipe off those tears ? Go along now, whoops! I've got business in hand . . .

Exit WELLESLEY (*who has shed no tears*). BLOMAX *addresses the audience.*

Far too much business, as a matter of fact. But the Emperor has commanded: I must follow his behests.

He leaves the stage to re-enter directly.

SCENE FIVE

The Police headquarters.
Stage divided into inner and outer offices. LUMBER *and the* PCs *occupy the outer office.*

WIPER *enters the inner office* (*from within*), *takes off his coat,*

sits down, covers his face with a red handkerchief and goes to sleep.
   BLOMAX *enters the outer office.*

BLOMAX. Hello, hello, hello, Sergeant Lumber, here we are
   again. Another day dawns and a lovely day for all.

LUMBER. Is it? I may say I'm extremely surprised to see *you*
   here, Dr Blomax. I've just been getting out a summons in
   your name. You've saved me the effort of sending a man
   round with it. Here you are, take it.

BLOMAX. Thank you very much . . . I'm going back by way of
   the Town Hall; I'll take the others as well, if you like, and
   save you some more effort.

LUMBER. Take what others, Dr Blomax? There's only one
   other – for the landlord of the Victoria and Albert, and it's
   already been served.

BLOMAX. Ah . . .

LUMBER. You might very well say 'Ah'.

BLOMAX (*gesturing towards the inner door*). Will he see me?

LUMBER. He won't.

BLOMAX. Ah . . . if I was to walk through, would you stop me
   by force?

LUMBER. I might have a try.

BLOMAX. I'm a stronger man than you are, and I can show you
   the proof.

   *He takes a banknote out of his pocket, furtively, taking care
   that the P Cs cannot see it.*

LUMBER. Oh no you can't. I wor proper insulted last night and
   my uniform humiliated. It's not that easy forgotten.

WIPER. Lumber!

LUMBER. Sir?

WIPER. I thought I told you I wasn't to be disturbed!

BLOMAX (*sings*).
                I married my wife because I had to
                Diddle di doo, di doo doo-doo . . .

WIPER *comes to the door.*

WIPER. I've nowt to say to you. I don't know who you are.

BLOMAX (*showing him the summons*). Oh yes, you do, Alfred. Because you've written me a letter. Why, I've got it in my hand. Look.

He slips past into the inner office.

WIPER (*coming in after him*). Sergeant Lumber, will you ask the Doctor to remove himself, please.

BLOMAX. Oh no, no, Alfred. We must look at this strategically.

He shuts the door. LUMBER *and the* PCs *withdraw into their own office.*

WIPER. Well?

BLOMAX. Only two summonses, Alfred . . .

WIPER. How many more did you want?

BLOMAX. Another couple o' pair might not have been inappropriate.

WIPER. They've sent you down here to find out the odds, isn't that so? Well, I can tell you straight now: the odds is black dangerous. And it doesn't please me any more than it does you. You talk about strategy: I've been using *tactics* – at the risk of my career – to save a few faces. I've been compelled to issue that one: and the one for the landlord, as a means of a cover . . . but look how I've worked it. Who do you think's going to be on the bench when you come up afore it?

BLOMAX. I dunno, who is?

WIPER. It *could* be Sir Harold Sweetman, and then you'd be i' t' cart . . . but as it so happens it'll be Alderman Butterthwaite. You're both going to plead guilty. You'll both be let off with a conditional discharge, and no further questions. There you are, tell your pals that, and bring me back their gratitude.

BLOMAX. Oh, very good, Alfred. Very tactical indeed. But it's not quite enough. They want to know in the Town Hall how far this is going and what it portends. In other words, they know your Colonel Feng is a most intrepid pioneer, but who gave him the notion that the best place to demonstrate his sterling British pluck was the Victoria and Albert on Uncle Charlie's Committee night.

WIPER. I don't believe that anybody gave it him.

BLOMAX. Oh yes, they did. We find ourselves here, sir, at a most surgical crux. We probe into it and we cut . . .

WIPER. And all that we discover is a magnificent backbone!

BLOMAX. You mean that he's entirely impartial!

WIPER. I am very sorry to tell you he is – absolutely impartial. A pub is a pub, a man is a drunken fornicator, and an Act of Parliament is divinity!

BLOMAX. Does that make you happy?

WIPER. It does not. For one thing, although I can't call myself an enthusiastic adherent of your horny-handed gang of trade-union oligarchs, at least for some years I have managed to retain a reasonably comfortable relationship with them. That is to say, I never interfered with their evening arrangements, and they never interfered with me.

BLOMAX. Until in walked the backbone . . . eh?

(*He sings.*)

> There came a ramrod vertebrae
> And its name was Colonel Feng.
> It pointed neither left nor right
> But strictly in between,
> And like a rattling bren gun, sir,
> This song he used to sing,
> That he cared for nobody, no, not he,
> And nobody cared for him!

WIPER. Do you have to do that in here?

BLOMAX. Of course, me dear Alfred, the comfort of your relationship has not been entirely confined to the trade-union oligarchs, has it? The word 'fornicator' was significant. What about the Copacabana Club?

WIPER. I do not understand you.

BLOMAX. No? If you were an honest law-man, you'd have closed that libidinous knocking-shop a long long time ago. Instead of which you've been paid to let it wriggle on. And who have you been paid by? The manageress. And how has she paid you? In kind, my dear Alfred. And very likely in cash. Though maybe not her own cash. It would be nice to know whose? I'm going to do it again, same tune, different words:

(*He sings.*)

> Big Gloria is a gorgeous girl
> And keeps many more employed
> Whose gorgeous curves for gorgeous money
> Are frequently enjoyed,
> And where and how that money goes
> Is fruitless to inquire,
> For bare and fruitless ever must be
> The fruits of man's desire.

WIPER. *Don't* start on a third stanza.

BLOMAX. You see, our Gloria herself's a patient of mine. She came to me last night for an abortion. *Your abortion*, Alfred . . . If she'd read her calendar correctly. But not being unaware of me medical ethics, I refused her request . . . at least for the time being. I never act precipitately. I always prefer to know just how it all sets up.

WIPER. I'll tell you how it all sets up. I'm a married man!

BLOMAX. Oh yes, I know that . . .

WIPER. And by God, why couldn't the stupid strumpet keep her purple mouth shut!

BLOMAX. Gloria and I are very old friends. And let me inform you, Alfred, she feels badly done to. However, however, keep your spirits hearty. It's not at all a bad thing I should know about all this, because I fancy I can help you.

LUMBER (*looking in briefly*). Excuse me, sir. You said to warn you, it's nearly ten to twelve.

He withdraws again.

WIPER. What! Oh, good heavens, get out of here quick! I'm expecting the Chief Constable at dead on the hour. If he should find you . . .

BLOMAX. No, no, no. Wait, Alfred. You and I are comfortable men, and we don't want to be disrupted. But if Colonel Feng is as impartial as you make out, and the Victoria and Albert was raided last night, not to embarrass the Labour Party, but out of pure zeal for good order: then he's not going to stop at embarrassing his own police force, nor yet the good people who pay for your inactivity. He's going to get you caught, and Gloria caught, and what's more her mysterious backers – who I'll bet are *not* disciples of Karl Marx or Keir Hardie.

WIPER. Aye, very likely. But I've not got time now. Will you please go, before we get trapped!

BLOMAX. But supposing – now listen, I am strategical – supposing Charlie Butterthwaite was to come to believe that Feng is *not* impartial, but a creature of Sweetman's, that he sent your lads to the pub to stir a political stink, then Charlie and his comrades are going to set right about and commence their *own* stirring. There will really be a stink, Feng will be sacked, or else forced to resign, and all disruption will be concluded before it touches *you*.

WIPER. It's a point, it's a point, I'll grant you it's a point . . . but will you please . . .

BLOMAX. It's a point well worth making . . .

VOICE (*off*). Ten-shun!

FENG (*off*). Good morning. Carry on, if you please.

LUMBER. Oh my Lord, he's here. Sir, sir, he's here!

FENG *enters the outer office.*

FENG. Good morning, Sergeant. Carry on. Superintendent in ?
LUMBER. Oh yessir, he's in, but . . .

FENG *passes through into the inner office.*

WIPER. Good morning, sir.
FENG. Good morning, Superintendent. I'm sorry if I'm a little early. Carry on, if you please.
WIPER. The gentleman's just going, sir.
BLOMAX (*singing to himself*).

> A babe of shame of such ill fame
> All it wants is an honest name
> Diddle di doo, di doo doo-doo . . .

He tips his hat to FENG *and goes out through the outer office.*

FENG. Who the devil's that ?
WIPER. Dr Wellington Blomax.
FENG. Who ?
WIPER. Dr Wellington Blomax, sir . . . A very brilliant practitioner, I believe . . . but of late years perhaps . . . er, h'm, he sometimes does our medical work for us.
FENG. Really ?
WIPER. Only occasionally, of course, when the regular man's away . . .
FENG. Superintendent, what steps are you taking to control the growth of organized vice in the borough.
WIPER. Fortunately very few, sir . . . I mean there are very few to take . . . We closed down a show at the Theatre Royal last year, the odd naughty girl still tries to advertise in the newsagent's windows, but we keep a close check. By and large, it's a clean community. The North of England, you know, the old puritanical traditions . . .
FENG. Good. I have a few notions of my own that it might be as well to look into, one of these days . . . quite soon, in fact. Yes. What about next Monday ?

WIPER. Next Monday, sir ? What . . . ?

FENG. Yes. Monday night. Send two or three plain clothes men to that place they call the Copacabana and find out what goes on . . . Any results of interest from your pub crawl, by the way ?

WIPER. Nothing of importance, sir, no . . . we've issued a couple of summonses . . . it is as well, however, to keep people reminded ?

FENG. It most certainly is, Superintendent. I know no attitude more corrupting to an efficient police force than that of complacency. I detect certain traces of it in your conversation; extirpate them, sir, extirpate them root and branch.

Exit FENG *through* WIPER's *inner door.*

WIPER. It can't be done, there's no time . . . besides, I don't trust that Doctor. I mean, I ask you, would *you* ? I shall have to *work* it on Monday. I shall have to work it the old way – that means by forewarning them – and it's never a safe way. I don't know what . . .

FENG (*within*). Superintendent ?

WIPER. Sir ?

FENG (*within*). Will you bring me the file upon last year's crimes of violence, please ?

WIPER. Sir, right away . . .

FENG (*within*). *And* the year before that, Superintendent, if you please . . .

Exeunt

SCENE SIX

BLOMAX's *surgery.*

Enter BLOMAX *and* GLORIA.

BLOMAX (*to audience*). I see very little reason why I should help

Alfred Wiper out of his self-created midden. Except my permanent necessity to have at least *one* copper bound to me by an obligation. And besides: I'm fond of Gloria.

(*He sings*):

The days they have been in the green of my garden
When between us was neither a 'beg your pardon'
Nor a 'stop it', nor 'give over': but 'here I am, here',
'Oh my dove and my dear', 'so close and so near'.
The days they have been, without forethought nor fear.

I'm sorry to keep you waiting, but I thought it'd be better to leave it till all the other patients were finished with. Tact, you know, discretion . . .

He examines her, cursorily, while talking.

GLORIA. Well, have you changed your mind ? Are you going to arrange it then ?

BLOMAX. Oh dear me, no. With this unprecedented Feng, a-prowling round the tent of Midian, illegal operations are very definitely *out*.

GLORIA. I see.

BLOMAX. Now look here, Gloria. Tell me truly. Who wants it ? You or Wiper ?

GLORIA. I thought you would ha' realized. I'm in a difficult position. I hold this job on a very tight contract and one of the clauses states that I must remain a woman of good reputation.

BLOMAX. Good reputation, in a joint like yours ?

GLORIA. Of course. It's a capital investment. It's got to be safeguarded.

BLOMAX. Any more dizzy spells, by the way ? Little vomitings ? Any o' that ?

GLORIA. No.

BLOMAX. Good girl, if you have a recurrence, take two o' these in water . . . (*He gives her some pills.*) But I just wish you could tell me whose capital it is.

GLORIA. Why?

BLOMAX. Because I think I ought to know. I need full possession of the facts. I'm trying to organize a political embranglement with the principal motive of keeping you out of jail. I tell you, Feng's prowling! The father of the son is a somewhat haunted Superintendent just at present, and he's afraid that he may not be able to give you value for your money for very much longer. He and I between us will do our level best to keep the flat feet of the law from pulverizing your terrazzo. But if we can't work it . . . be ready, and be warned.

GLORIA. You mean, I suppose, he'll have to raid the club.

BLOMAX. Something after that fashion. But no doubt he'll give you notice. All I say is: be ready.

GLORIA. Principal motive, eh? Keep me out of jail? Oh no, come clean. What is it you're after?

BLOMAX. After? But I *told* you—

GLORIA. I've known you too long. You *enjoy* your embranglements, don't you. You set them up on purpose. Just like with Charlie Butterthwaite and all them bets you let him lose, but you wouldn't dream of foreclosing. So long as all your friends are still standing under obligations to you, you've got something to live for . . . I don't want this baby. All right. What's to happen?

BLOMAX. What indeed? Oh dearie me, what indeed, indeed . . .

> It is not alone my friends
> Who stand under an obligation,
> I too have a duty, Gloria,
> In view of our past relation.
> You wish me to preserve it,
> And I will: your reputation:
> It runs tick-tock, tick-tock,
> At the core of my cogitation.

It's only a matter of days now, I have to go to Beverley to the races. Why don't you come with me?

GLORIA. I wouldn't be seen dead.

BLOMAX. At least as far as Doncaster. I can fix it up at the Office there. I know a man in the Office . . .

GLORIA. What Office?

BLOMAX. In Doncaster. You'll find out. Oh dearie me, what a curious prescription. But legal, I think it's legal . . . Come on, cheery-up . . . and the corners of your mouth, dear, let them lift, let them lift!

He breaks into a song and forces her to dance with him. She does so unwillingly at first, but then laughs and they are gay.

> I look to the left
> And I look to the right
> I'm a dirty old devil
> Alone in the notions
>
> Of politics and progress
> And high-minded soaring
> With a little bit to drink
> And a slice of good hope
>
> For my patients
> And a smile and bright word
> And don't you go thinking
> You can call me a tortoise
>
> And a dormouse
> And a ostrich in sand
> If it ever gets too hot
> I can pull out my hand
> I can pull out my hand
> I can pull out my hand . . .

Exeunt

SCENE SEVEN

A room in the Town Hall.

LEFTWICH *enters with a loaded tea trolley and starts arranging cups and saucers.* BLOMAX *enters from the side opposite his last exit, carrying a black bag.*

BLOMAX. Good afternoon, Constable Leftwich retired.

LEFTWICH. Afternoon, Doctor.

BLOMAX. The Town Hall seems strangely empty. Is it not three o'clock yet?

LEFTWICH. Five minutes after. Town Planning Committee's in session today. As you know, His Worship takes a very close interest there, and he never were the swiftest to elucidate a technical agenda.

BLOMAX. Aye . . . How's his leg?

LEFTWICH. Nay . . .

BLOMAX. I thought so. I've brought the doings. (*He lays his bag on the trolley.*) What about Uncle Charlie? Is he at the Town Planning?

LEFTWICH. He isn't. He's down at t'Rates Office. Creating with the clerks. One of the accountants discovered a discrepancy and there's a fair foaming fury going on about it, I can tell you.

BLOMAX. That could be very timely. I'll nip down and intercept him before he cools off.

He is about to go out when he is prevented by the entrance of MRS BOOCOCK. *He makes a leg.*

Good afternoon, Madam Mayoress. Once again the sun rises upon our matutinal gloom and fog, and once again in your presence . . .

MRS BOOCOCK. Good afternoon, Dr Blomax. Herbert, where's the Mayor? Is he still wi' t'Town Planning?

Exit BLOMAX *disappointed.*

LEFTWICH. They should be out for a breather any time now.

MRS BOOCOCK. They'd better be. They've been stuck wi' that traffic roundabout for the best part of two months.

LEFTWICH. Here they are, they're coming . . .

Enter BOOCOCK *and* LABOUR COUNCILLORS. *They sit down, exhausted, to their tea.*

BOOCOCK. Ah . . . hello, Sarah love. How are you ? Well, at last we look like coming to some sort of conclusion. But the amount o' vested interest involved in this one item . . . Oh, I do wish Charlie wor sitting in on this. *He'd* sort us out all right. What's happened to him today ?

LEFTWICH. Rates Office.

BOOCOCK. Oh, that . . .

HARDNUTT. What's he got to do wi' t'Rates Office, for God-sake ? It's none o' his department. He can't keep his nose out, can he ?

HOPEFAST. I thought we paid a permanent staff to deal with all that.

BOOCOCK. The permanent staff are responsible to the demo-cratic representatives.

HOPEFAST. All right, Barney, we know. But some of them representatives sometimes seem to forget that they bloody well *are* democratic.

HICKLETON. I don't think we should begrudge him his little investigations. He's only cooking up the books for his summer holidays, I dare say.

BOOCOCK. He's *what* ?

HICKLETON. Just a joke . . .

BOOCOCK. Well, I don't call it funny. That's the sort of humour, fellow Councillor, that gets reported out of walls. Remember there's men in this town . . . aye, and in this building . . . if we give them so much as one crook of a

finger they will turn it back on to us like a bloody harpoon.
And that's not what we're chosen for.

> I will not have it dreamed or thought
> Or even in a whisper told
> That any man of our good men
> Can wear the shameful label:
> 'Bought and Sold'.
> We're up here to show the Tories
> How honest men can rule.
> We've a built a playground for the little children
> And a comprehensive school.
> We lead the whole West Riding
> In our public schemes of housing,
> And for the drainage of the town,
> In pre-stressed concrete firm and strong
> That not an H-bomb can ding down,
> The Borough Engineer's contrived
> A revolutionary outfall:
> And add to that we've built
> This splendid new Town Hall.

He sits down in pain.

> It comes a rugged reflection
> To a rude old man like me
> Who's had no ease to his efforts
> Nor helpful education:
> That in the hour of his honour
> And the heaping of red robes
> And gold chains of his glory
> He sets up a strong staircase
> For to stride up in his pride:
> And reaches nowt but rheumatics
> Nosing theirselves northward
> From his knee to his ribcage!

MRS BOOCOCK. He's often short of money. I've heard that for a fact.

BOOCOCK. We're all often short.

MRS BOOCOCK. Oh no, not *you*. Economically regulated, aye, but you can't say I keep you short.

BOOCOCK. That's not to the purpose. We're talking about Charlie.

MRS BOOCOCK. Aye, the famous nine-times Mayor . . . or are you sure it isn't ten?

BOOCOCK. I am the Mayor, Sarah.

MRS BOOCOCK. You wear the chain.

BOOCOCK. I hold the office!

MRS BOOCOCK. The office of what? He's selected you this season to play the centre-forward in his own private football team, but don't you imagine that gives you any control over fixture-lists, transfer-fees, or owt else o' t'manager's business!

BOOCOCK. My God, she's never been to a football match in her life.

MRS BOOCOCK. All right and I haven't. They call me Madam Mayoress and I belong in t'kitchen to mash you your tea and fry up your bacon, but happen I might wonder who really owns the belly where it lodges on its road. That's all, I say no more . . .

Enter BUTTERTHWAITE *and* BLOMAX.

BUTTERTHWAITE. I *knew* it. I knew it in here! (*He thumps his belly.*) The predictable result is this of not consulting *me*! My gallstones weren't that bad, I could ha' . . .

BLOMAX. Alfred Wiper said to me . . .

BUTTERTHWAITE. Don't you talk to me about Wiper. There's only one thing fit to be wiped off by that wedge o' greasy gammon and that's his own fat clarted . . . ha, h'm, watch our language . . .

MRS BOOCOCK. Gammon, bacon, or ham: it's time it were took off its hook. It's oversmoked and downright nasty.

Exit MRS BOOCOCK.

BUTTERTHWAITE. Have you heard what Wellington said, Barney?

BOOCOCK. No, I have not.

BUTTERTHWAITE. That business last night at the Victoria and Albert were a well-planned put-up job organized by Sweetman, for the discredit of Labour. And if it warn't for the degenerate meanderings of Superintendent Alfred Wiper, they'd ha' succeeded and all!

BOOCOCK. It sounds highly unlikely to me. Colonel Feng's only been here for nigh on . . .

BUTTERTHWAITE. What the hell does it matter how long he's been here! All that we're concerned with now is how soon he gets out!

The COUNCILLORS *suck their teeth and look doubtful.*

BOOCOCK. You know perfectly well, Charlie Butterthwaite, that you were all boozing after hours. If you got yourselves into trouble you've only yourselves to thank. I will not have aspersions cast upon an unproven public servant. He were doing nowt more nor demonstrating his efficiency, and . . .

BUTTERTHWAITE. Barney, he was striking directly at *me*. It was not only political, it was bloody well personal. And I want him done with!

BOOCOCK. I will not discuss it further. Will you take a look at my leg, Doctor; it's been acting up again.

BLOMAX *kneels and examines the leg.*

BUTTERTHWAITE. Barney, I don't think you quite understand the realities at issue. In our party and our principles, upon which we stand four-square – do we or don't we?—

COUNCILLORS. We do.

BUTTERTHWAITE. – we are confronted with a crisis upon a national scale. Is Labour, or is Labour not, to find a triumphant resurgence? I hope so. So do you.

BLOMAX. Quite a normal stiffening, I think. I'll send some more embrocation.

BUTTERTHWAITE. But no effort in Westminster is worth a damn thing by itself without a sound rammed foundation in the provincial localities. And as far as this locality is concerned if we permit the Tories to fix our police force, we're on t'first road in to mucky marsh, and your old Uncle Charlie knows it. Am I right, fellow Councillors?

COUNCILLORS. Aye . . . I dare say . . . I wouldn't dispute it. . . etc.

BUTTERTHWAITE. Mr Mayor, am I right?

BOOCOCK. It may well be as you say. But if we sack a Chief Constable on inadequate grounds the Home Secretary can withdraw the Government grant from the finances of our Watch Committee. And then who's going to pay for keeping the pavements safe from cosh-boys? You? Out of *your* winnings? Don't make me laugh. We'd best get back to Committee. Doctor, would you mind just giving me an arm as we walk down the corridor; it's not quite eased off yet. Come on, you'll be late.

Exit BOOCOCK *with* BLOMAX. *The* COUNCILLORS *move to follow him.*

BUTTERTHWAITE. If there is a police traffic officer giving advice on that roundabout, just you treat him distant. I want them to know that I know what I know.

COUNCILLORS. Aye . . . Well . . . we'll see how it turns out . . . etc.

Exeunt COUNCILLORS.

BUTTERTHWAITE. Upon inadequate grounds. All right. Make 'em adequate . . . Lend me ten bob, will you?

LEFTWICH. What, me? Are you mad?

BUTTERTHWAITE. Constable Leftwich, it's a generation or two since you last trod the beat, but nevertheless you are wearing the uniform. Declare yourself, Leftwich! Commit your allegiance! (*He offers* LEFTWICH *a pocket flask.*)

LEFTWICH. Commit it to what?

BUTTERTHWAITE. To the Council of this town in democracy assembled or else – and I shan't take it kindly if you choose the alternative – to the oppressive bonds and authoritarian regiment of a crypto-fascist police organization! Which?

LEFTWICH. Do I have to choose either?

BUTTERTHWAITE. You do, lad, you do. Because as from this moment a state of formal war exists. Come on, now. Commit yourself.

LEFTWICH (*drinking*). I know where my bread's buttered. It's buttered in *here* . . .

BUTTERTHWAITE *takes the bottle and drinks.*

BUTTERTHWAITE. Barney won't play, and this one's too important for fiddling it behind his back. So we can't get Feng directly. What we're going to do is to employ his own tactics. Discredit him by discrediting the behaviour of his troops.

LEFTWICH. Now just you be careful. Why not leave it settle for a little while longer?

BUTTERTHWAITE. I have been struck at! Directly! In person! Herbert, I want some secrets. Who pays the top bogeys how much for keeping quiet about what?

LEFTWICH. I couldn't really say. It used to be the tarts, but since the new Act come in I've lost all me locations in *that* corner o' wickedness.

BUTTERTHWAITE. I want summat deeper. But I think we're on t'right lines . . .

LEFTWICH. Copacabana?

BUTTERTHWAITE. Naked dancing? . . . Maybe . . . but just

how rude is it ? And what evidence is there that the police are
conniving at it ?

LEFTWICH. As far as I know there's none. Except that big
Gloria's been to bed with Alfred Wiper.

BUTTERTHWAITE. Who told you that!

LEFTWICH. My brother-in-law's a window-cleaner, and he
looks at what he sees.

BUTTERTHWAITE. I suppose he didn't look far enough to find
out where t'money comes from . . . I mean, that club's new
builded, it must ha' cost a lot o' brickwork.

LEFTWICH. Who were t'contractors ? 'Durable Construction',
warn't it ?

BUTTERTHWAITE. Aye . . . now they also put up a new malt-
house for Harry Sweetman two year sin'. It proves bloody
little, but we *are* on t'right lines . . . I think it's high time I
betrayed the working classes, don't you ? And patronized an
entertainment that is normally above my means. (*He consults
his diary.*) I've nowt on next Monday. What about Monday ?
All right then, write it down, the Copacabana, Monday. And
we'll see what shape of others have got nowt on on that
evening. Ha, ha. You watch me conquer yet again where few
will follow and none will praise me till I do it, and then
they'll all fall on their knees !

He sings, with LEFTWICH *joining in the refrain.*

O Boney came from Corsica, oh hi oh,
He conquered the penisula, John Franzwo.
He went and beat the Prooshians, oh hi oh,
And then he beat the Rooshians, John Franzwo.
Boney was a General, oh hi oh,
And then he was Imperial, John Franzwo.
Boney was a warrior, oh hi oh,
Begod he was no tarrier, John Franzwo.

*And so on, dancing round in a circle, drinking their whisky,
then exeunt*

SCENE EIGHT

Outside the Copacabana Club.
Night.
Enter BUTTERTHWAITE *and Labour Councillors.*

BUTTERTHWAITE. A preliminary reekin-ayssance. Who'll be the first to enter the portals of iniquity and see how the other half lusts?

HOPEFAST. I expect we'll have to be members.

HARDNUTT. It'll cost us at least a quid apiece, you know.

BUTTERTHWAITE. Out of the party funds, lad. It's a delegated investigation, this. And I'll answer to the secretary if there's any questions asked . . . Lend me five bob, will you? We'll have to buy a beer if we're going to look natural. Come on, lad, come on! Who paid for the taxi from the Victoria and Albert?

    HARDNUTT *gives him the money.*

Right, we'll go in.

    They approach the entrance and the DOORMAN *appears.*

DOORMAN. Evening, gentlemen. Members?

BUTTERTHWAITE. We're not, but we can be. What does it cost?

DOORMAN. Eighty-five shillings renewable annually. Membership, however, does not take effect till twenty-four hours after payment of first subscription.

BUTTERTHWAITE. You mean we can't get in here while tomorrow night! Why, we might all be blown up first thing i' t'morning! My lad, at this very moment the generals of the Western world are stooping over t'map tables, the mill-wheel of our lifetime is whirling under spate! . . . Now come off it, sonny Jack. You know damn well if we'd just arrived in

town on a one-day business conference you'd have opened
up directly.

DOORMAN. Not unless you had a sponsor, I'm afraid, sir . . .

> BUTTERTHWAITE *signals to* HARDNUTT, *who fiddles with
> his wallet.*

But it's not at all impossible that something could be
managed . . . Just one moment, if you please . . . (*He dis-
appears inside.*)

BUTTERTHWAITE. See what I mean? They're breaking the
law already. Note the time.

> *The* DOORMAN *reappears.*

DOORMAN. You're fortunate, sir. A lady inside has offered to
be your sponsor. So if you'll just sign the book . . .

> HARDNUTT *passes money to* BUTTERTHWAITE, *who
> passes over tip.*

Thank you very much, sir, indeed, sir, very much . . . Now,
eighty-five shillings multiplied by four, exactly seventeen
pounds . . . and entrance fee five shillings each makes
eighteen pounds precisely . . .

> HARDNUTT *pays him.*

Thank you, gentlemen. Straight forward if you please . . .
Thank you very much.

> *They enter the club*

SCENE NINE

Inside the Copacabana Club.

*Not many customers at tables. Waitresses in brief versions of
Flamenco skirts. A few hostesses in evening gowns. Latin American
music. A pseudo-Spanish dance-routine taking place on the small
stage.* YOUNG SWEETMAN (*drunk*) *at a table with a hostess.*

BUTTERTHWAITE *and* COUNCILLORS *advance into the room. They are shown to a table.*

BUTTERTHWAITE. We'll have a Guinness and a double Scotch to go with it.

WAITRESS. We don't serve Guinness, I'm afraid, sir.

BUTTERTHWAITE. You don't? Then you ought to. It'd put a bit o' blood under that nice white hide o' yourn, lass. Heh heh. What *do* you serve?

WAITRESS. Certainly whisky.

BUTTERTHWAITE. That's a bit o' good tidings, any road.

WAITRESS. But I'm afraid there's no drinks allowed without something to eat.

HARDNUTT. We don't want nowt to eat. We had us suppers already.

WAITRESS. It doesn't need more than a sandwich, you know.

HOPEFAST. All right then, four sandwiches.

HICKLETON. We don't have to have a sandwich every time we refill, do we? It's too much like hard work.

WAITRESS. Not unless you want to.

BUTTERTHWAITE. All right. And look sharp, love, won't you? We're evaporating in this heat. (WAITRESS *leaves them.*) Place seems a bit empty. They can hardly make it pay at this rate of attendance, can they?

HARDNUTT. I dare say the fancy don't come in while after midnight.

BUTTERTHWAITE. Aye, very likely.

HICKLETON (*watching a hostess*). Eh, do you reckon *she's* one on 'em?

BUTTERTHWAITE. I'd not be surprised . . . Hey up, she's coming over.

HOSTESS *approaches them.*

HOPEFAST. Now then, Charlie, watch it. We're disinterested observers.

BUTTERTHWAITE. Disinterested bloody slag-ladles. We're

full members of this joint and we're going to take advantage
. . . Go on, love, have a chair. Get the weight off your thigh-
bones?

She sits down at their table.

HOSTESS. I don't mind if I do.

BUTTERTHWAITE. What are you drinking?

HOSTESS. I'd like a tomato juice if you please, Alderman.

BUTTERTHWAITE. Eh, she knows who I am! There's some in
this town pay proper respect where it ought to be paid. Take
a bit o' note, you lot . . . but you're wanting summat
warmer nor tomato juice . . . surely? Put a bit o' blood
under that nice white hide, you know? Go on, love . . . have
a glass o' gin.

HOSTESS. Call it a Babycham. I've got work to do.

She makes a signal to the WAITRESS.

BUTTERTHWAITE. Ho ho, have you, ducky, have you? That's
what I like to hear, the craftsmanship approach, very good,
eh? Ho ho, work to do . . .

HICKLETON (*watching the dancers, who are varying their
routine*). Eh, Charlie, what about that?

BUTTERTHWAITE *makes a lecherous noise.*

What do you think, is she going to get 'em all ripped off?

YOUNG SWEETMAN (*lurching towards them*). What do *you*
think, Councillor? Wouldn't you like to have a go at her
yourself, eh?

YOUNG SWEETMAN'S HOSTESS (*restraining him*). Come on,
love, behave.

YOUNG SWEETMAN. Why shouldn't I behave? I represent
the standards of civilization in this paleo-paleo-paleolithicalo-
lithealithic community. I've had an education.

He subsides into his HOSTESS's *lap.*

BUTTERTHWAITE. My God, you have an' all . . . I imagine, though, we have to wait while end of the evening for t'right spice o' t'show.

HOSTESS. Not tonight you don't.

HOPEFAST. Not? Why not?

HOSTESS. Haven't you heard? There's going to be a raid.

BUTTERTHWAITE. A raid? You don't mean the police?

HOSTESS. That's right.

HARDNUTT. Oh my Lord, no . . .

HOPEFAST. I say, Charlie, that's gone and torn it, hasn't it?

BUTTERTHWAITE. Has it? I'm not sure . . . How do you know there's going to be a raid?.

HOSTESS. I don't know exactly. The warning just came. Gloria said she was passing it round all the members who might not want their names in the paper. Just in case something was to go wrong, you know. But you see, we were told that there'd be no danger before midnight, so there's nothing really to worry about. We're having all the popular routines now, and after twelve o'clock there'll be nothing but ordinary vocal numbers and dancing to the band and all that. We'd hoped the place would be as full as usual but a bit earlier on, but it looks like they all took fright, doesn't it?

BUTTERTHWAITE. They'd take fright in this town if a centipede ran ower t'road. Get their names i' t'papers! They think it's worse nor doing murder! Ah well, we won't worry. We're getting some o' what we paid for. We can allus come again.

HARDNUTT (*who has been given the bill*). Can we, by God? Take a look at this!

BUTTERTHWAITE. And they call this a sandwich! It's not even got a top on. (*As the* WAITRESS *is going away*.) Hey up, love! We want a Babycham for t'young lady.

HOSTESS. It's all right, she's brought it.

BUTTERTHWAITE. But I never ordered it yet.

HOSTESS. Oh, just the telegraph . . .

HARDNUTT. Damned expensive telegraph . . . fifteen and six for one Babycham, Charlie!

BUTTERTHWAITE (*watching the dance*). Shut up, lad, I'm watching summat. Use a bit of aesthetic appreciation, or else get off home. I'm here to enjoy meself. (*He cuddles the* HOSTESS.) Eh, what, me little sweetheart? Every man's entitled to his own Dolce Vita, isn't that the truth?

HOSTESS. Aye, lad, it's the truth.

BUTTERTHWAITE (*becoming uproarious*). It's the buttock-naked truth! (*He shouts to the performers, who are near the end of the act.*) Go on, tear it off, I want to see the lot!

Blackout. Lights come up. The Club stage is now empty. GLORIA *is standing beside* BUTTERTHWAITE.

GLORIA. Control yourself, Alderman, this isn't the cattle market . . . Can I join you in a whisky? Cost price for the Corporation. (*She waves to the* WAITRESS, *then points to the bill.*) Don't you pay that. You're honoured guests tonight. (*To the* HOSTESS.) Marlene, you ought to ha' warned me. I warn't to expect we'd be entertaining royalty. As a matter of fact, we warn't to expect that the royalty would be likely to find this a congenial establishment. We tend to cater for what you might call the . . .

BUTTERTHWAITE. The acquisitive and the affluent. Ah, the caterpillars o' the boss class. *I* know, I've said it all. But between what we say and what we find congenial . . .

HOPEFAST. You see, we did damn well at Beverley Races this afternoon.

HICKLETON. Did we?

BUTTERTHWAITE. We did. We made a killing. And now we're out to find ourselves some carnal satisfaction.

GLORIA. So I hope we can provide it for you. Though it's forced to be a bit curtailed tonight.

BUTTERTHWAITE. Aye, aye, she's explained already. (*Four dancing girls, one pair dressed in balloons, the other pair in little*

bells, appear on the club stage. Nude tableau behind. After a
short dance on stage they come down among the tables.) Hello,
hello, hello, what do we do wi' these?

DANCERS. Poppety pop, pop a balloon . . . ring a ding, ding,
ring a little bell.

Audience participation.

BUTTERTHWAITE. Pop.
HICKLETON. Pop.
BUTTERTHWAITE. Ding-a-ding.
HICKLETON. Ding-a-ding . . . etc.

An electric bell suddenly rings loudly. The DOORMAN *comes
in shouting 'Twelve o'clock Midnight'. The Dancing girls
hurry off. Tableau closes.* BUTTERTHWAITE *and the*
COUNCILLORS *are left in the middle of the floor. The band
starts to play 'The Blue Danube'.* YOUNG SWEETMAN *is
three parts insensible and his* HOSTESS *tries in vain to get
him to move.*

GLORIA. Won't you dance, then, Alderman? (*She begins to
waltz with him, and other couples follow suit.*)

BUTTERTHWAITE. Me dance . . . ho ho, dance. *I'll* give you a
dance! (*To band.*) Quicken it up, lads; can't you see we're
leaving you behind! (*Music changes to a Tango.*) That's a bit
more like it! *One* two three four, *one* two three four, etc . . .

LUMBER *and a* PC (*in plain clothes*) *enter and sit down at a
table. The dancing fades away.* BUTTERTHWAITE *points at
them and leers.*

    If you ever walk down our street
    You will see a right pretty seet,
    All the policemen four five six
    A-knocking on the doors with big black sticks!

LUMBER. Do you think we could have half a pint of bitter beer
apiece, please, miss?

WAITRESS. Oh no, I'm afraid not, you see it's after hours.

LUMBER. Yes, of course, it is, isn't it?

BUTTERTHWAITE. Go on, you give it to him. As a present, on the house! He's an agent provocative, but so long as it's clearly understood all round no harm need be done! Isn't that so, Sarn't Lumber?

LUMBER. I think we'll have a cup of coffee. And it wouldn't be a bad idea if certain other gentlemen present were introduced to that excellent drink.

> BUTTERTHWAITE *laughs.* YOUNG SWEETMAN *rises unsteadily, and tries to walk to the door. He staggers into* WIPER, *who has just come in, and who ignores him.*

WIPER. I'm sure we would all be glad to share the joke, Alderman.

BUTTERTHWAITE. And why not indeed? Would you call it a dirty joke? Pornographic? Indecent?

WIPER. I don't think so. Why should I?

BUTTERTHWAITE. Then what are you doing here? You tell me that.

WIPER. I am acting upon an information that the entertainment provided at these premises is of a nature liable to cause offence by reason of obscenity.

GLORIA. And is it?

WIPER. Sergeant?

LUMBER. Upon our arrival here, sir, dancing was in progress in a normal fashion. Men strictly dancing with women without undue proximity. There was no display of nakedness nor other indecent exhibition.

GLORIA. And the licensing laws, Sergeant?

LUMBER. Were being properly observed. Ha h'm.

> YOUNG SWEETMAN *finally effects his departure.*

WIPER. In that case it is evident that there are no grounds whatever for the bringing of charges. May I apologize, Madam, for an unfortunate error?

GLORIA. I'm sorry you've been troubled.

BUTTERTHWAITE. Wait a moment, wait a moment . . . As a magistrate and a leading citizen, *I* desire to lay an information against the conduct of this club.

GLORIA. Why, you cunning old . . .

BUTTERTHWAITE. We have just witnessed a demonstration of the passing about among the tables of four little doxies dressed in nowt but balloons – or, in the case of two of 'em, bells – which we were invited to burst or to tingle as the case may be. I am in no doubt whatever that had it not been for the approach of midnight – liberally signalled, I may say – they would have been rendered entirely naked within the handgrasp of the customer. There were other irregularities, too, which I will detail in due course. What are you going to do about it ?

WIPER. You, er – heard what the Sergeant said, Alderman. He observed no sign of . . .

BUTTERTHWAITE. Indeed he did not. Because you know and I know and our Gloria knows that the management had been forewarned.

COUNCILLORS. *And* we can corroborate it.

GLORIA. It's all a pack of lies ; it's an absolute frame-up.

WIPER. This is very serious indeed, and can only be gone into in the proper manner of procedure. Please attend my office in the morning. We can then discuss it in . . .

BUTTERTHWAITE. Oho no, none o' that patter, mate !

WIPER. I wouldn't advise you to try and be too rapid. I don't think it will pay off . . . Sergeant, come along.

> *Exeunt police. The dancers, etc., are now all on stage more or less dressed.*

BUTTERTHWAITE. Before you raging ladies come and scratch my eyesight out, I had better make one thing clear. I didn't come here to deprive you of your livelihoods. However, in the fell and calamitous grinding of two mighty opposites, someone has to go to t'wall. And them wi' fewest clothes on o' force gets squeezed hardest! Do all o' you girls belong to a union?

A GIRL. Most of us don't.

BUTTERTHWAITE. You don't? A pitiful state of affairs, which only goes to show how right I was to come here. Councillor Hopefast, will you make out a memo for the next meeting o' t'trades council, in re the possible affiliations for members of this industry. They're sweet and jetting little wildflies, and they deserve our firm attention.

(*He sings.*)

> When I was a young man in my prime
> Hoor ray Santy Anna
> I knocked them yeller gals two at a time
> All on the plains of Mexico!

He leads his COUNCILLORS *out, laughing grossly.*

GLORIA. All right, all out, we're closing, we're done for, clear it away, no evidence, nothing – my God that bloody old tup, but he'll get his horns curled yet!

Act Two

SCENE ONE

Sweetman's house.

Doorbell rings (off) SWEETMAN *in a dressing-gown hurries across the stage to answer it.* LADY SWEETMAN *in a dressing-gown comes in after him and stands listening.*

SWEETMAN *(off)*. Superintendent Wiper! At this time of night!

WIPER *(off)*. I'm sorry to disturb you, Sir Harold, but something very awkward . . . *(Mumble, mumble.)*

SWEETMAN *(off)*. What . . . what . . . Good God!

WIPER *(off)*. Do you think I could come in, sir? I mean it *is* rather . . .

SWEETMAN *(off)*. In? D'you mean 'in'? Just a moment, I . . . *(*SWEETMAN *re-enters.)* It's all right, my dear, it's nothing important . . . Would you mind going back to bed?

LADY SWEETMAN. Harold, I . . .

SWEETMAN. Bed, please. *If* you don't mind!

LADY SWEETMAN. Harold. Very well. *(She goes.)*

SWEETMAN *beckons in* WIPER.

SWEETMAN. How dare you come here, straight to this house!

WIPER. I had no alternative. I'm getting meself into a right pitchy mess-up looking after your interests.

SWEETMAN. My what did you say?

WIPER. We have never dealt together personally on this matter before, but the Copacabana is your private investment. And don't you try and deny it.

SWEETMAN. I most emphatically do deny . . .

WIPER. No, it won't do. You know perfectly well what goes on there, and who's been getting paid for keeping it protected. The time has now arrived for *you* to protect *me*. You're an Alderman and a magistrate, so use it to some purpose!

SWEETMAN. Yes . . . How much does Butterthwaite know?

WIPER. He knows that the police raid was established with collusion . . . Good God, he was told it straight by one o' those half-wit tarts! But I don't think he knows details and I don't think he knows about *your* concern, specific.

SWEETMAN. Was he drunk, by any chance?

WIPER. Drunk? I smelt a pong off all four of 'em like a streetful of breweries!

SWEETMAN. Breweries? Yes.

WIPER. Yes, well . . .

SWEETMAN. What was he doing? Precisely?

WIPER. Dancing the tango.

SWEETMAN. Wildly?

WIPER. Uproariously.

SWEETMAN. Then we'd better tell the Chief Constable. (*He goes towards the telephone.*) No. Wait. Have they been charged? I mean, for drunkenness, or the like?

WIPER. Not yet, no . . .

SWEETMAN. Then see that they are not. The accusations they have brought are, ha-hm, very wild indeed, and we are in considerable danger here of a first-class political row. Men of that type who have been in absolute power for over thirty years, why, they'd stick at nothing. We don't want to see a responsible public servant like Colonel Feng turned into a political shuttlecock. Do we? Get hold of all the other customers who were in the club this evening and get sworn affidavits as to the innocence of the show, and also, if you like, the hooliganism of Butterthwaite. Impress Colonel Feng with the hooliganism of Butterthwaite.

WIPER. What about the club itself?

SWEETMAN. Yes . . . I'll have to think of something. I may turn it to advantage . . . Yes. Good night, Superintendent.

As he shows him out, LADY SWEETMAN *re-enters.*
YOUNG SWEETMAN *enters and meets* WIPER.

YOUNG SWEETMAN. Oh my God, not here as well. Oh God, I'm off. (*He goes out again.*)

SWEETMAN. Maurice! You come back here, boy!

WIPER. I'm sorry about this, Sir Harold. I suppose you won't want me to take an affidavit off of *him*?

SWEETMAN. Was he there, too? . . . Good heavens . . . No, we can't risk exceptions, take his statement with the rest – in the morning. There are five steps to the front door. *Don't* miss your footing. Good night.

WIPER *goes out.* SWEETMAN *calls:*
Maurice!

Re-enter YOUNG SWEETMAN.

It's all right, he's gone. Now then: who were you there with? Blomax's girl?

YOUNG SWEETMAN. No.

SWEETMAN. Oh, weren't you? Astonishing . . . Has she not got you caught yet, then?

YOUNG SWEETMAN. Caught? Do you mean . . . ?

SWEETMAN. Yes, I damn well *do* mean it! Now I give you a fair choice, boy, leave her alone, or get out of my brewery. There's a great deal of villainy turning itself round in this town that you know nowt about. And think yourself lucky the police have done nothing more than warn me about you.

YOUNG SWEETMAN *goes in.*

Do you know what the time is?

LADY SWEETMAN. What did he want?

SWEETMAN. Who?

LADY SWEETMAN. The Superintendent.

SWEETMAN. Maurice. The boy was drunk.

LADY SWEETMAN. So I see . . . Can they send you to prison?

SWEETMAN. What . . . !

LADY SWEETMAN. I couldn't help overhearing. How deeply are you mixed up in it, Harold? Have you been bribing the police, have you been . . .

SWEETMAN. No. Emphatically! No. I have not! Now will you please go back to bed!

LADY SWEETMAN. I wish you weren't so bad-tempered. I'm only trying to . . .

SWEETMAN. I'm sorry. I didn't mean to be. No . . . but, er, it's just a return of the old bother, it makes me a bit edgy . . . (*He mimes a pain in his heart.*) I'll take a drop of medicine and come to bed when it settles . . . Go on, now. Happy dreams . . .

She goes, avoiding his embrace.

Happy dreams and sweet awakenings . . .
    It has been argued and by no less a voice
    Than that of the Prime Minister, that today
    Class-struggle is concluded. All can rise
    Or fall according to desire or merits
    Or (it may be) according to finance.
    I am as rich as any man in Yorkshire,
    I brew good beer and drink my own good product.
    I fabricate perfected breakfast food
    And crunch it with my family round my table.
    Both beer and breakfast food are drunk and crunched
    By simultaneous millions through the land.
    So Sweetman should have risen, so he has,
    But to what eminence? Financial, yes.
    And social: yes indeed. My wife has mink,
    My daughters, jewels and suitors: My three tall sons
    Inhabit, or have inhabited, public schools.
    They grow to love the world I set them in,
    And, loving it, become it as they walk.

I am a prince, I am a baron, sirs!
And yet I have no sovereignty, no.
For what is power of gold when politics
At every turn deceive my high aspiring?
The election lights on Butterthwaite – not once
But three times three, or nine times nine, I fear.
No national trend, nor local, gives me hope
Of an improvement. Yet Butterthwaite must fall
And fall so low that not the whole ineptitude
And hopelessness of Tory forecasts can
Reverse his long-delayed catastrophe.
He has himself prepared his own trap-door
And greased his easy hinge. Tonight, he did it!
All it needs now, cagy play and watch
For luck to rock the lock and heave the lever:
And he's down! Prison? . . . No, I do not think so . . .
I am too expert. And in their good time
I turn to the electorate and they turn
In *my* good time, to me! And turn for ever! Yes . . .

Exit

SCENE TWO

A room in the Town Hall.

Enter BOOCOCK, BUTTERTHWAITE *and* LABOUR COUN-
CILLORS.

BOOCOCK. This is very troublesome altogether, Charlie. I hope
you haven't gone too far.

BUTTERTHWAITE. I haven't, Barney.

BOOCOCK. Just how sozzled were you at the Copacabana,
Charlie?

BUTTERTHWAITE. At the Copacabana, Barney, I was as sober
as a chief constable. Isn't that the truth?

COUNCILLORS. Aye, it's the truth.

BUTTERTHWAITE. The buttock-naked truth!

BOOCOCK. I have no desire whatever to make a statement to the Press.

BUTTERTHWAITE. If you don't, I will.

BOOCOCK. I am quite sure that you will . . .

Enter JOURNALISTS.

Gentlemen, good morning. I am sorry you have been brought here. I have remarkably little to say. Except that it does appear that all is not well with the borough police force.

1ST JOURNALIST. Is it true, Mr Mayor, that the Copacabana Club . . . ?

BOOCOCK. I am naming no names.

2ND JOURNALIST. Have you discussed it with the Chief Constable?

1ST JOURNALIST. It is arguable, is it not, that the Chief Constable has the right to conduct his *own* investigation into matters concerning the . . .

BUTTERTHWAITE. I'll answer that, Barney. Now look here, young man. The police are public servants and responsible to the public!

1ST JOURNALIST. But surely the Home Secretary . . .

BUTTERTHWAITE. The Home Secretary's nowt to do wi' it! The Home Secretary's a Tory and he lives in bloody London! The Government here is *us*, and we're not satisfied. Mister Feng's police force is putrid with corruption and if he don't take a long-handled dung fork to it pretty damn quick, I want his resignation! What's more, I'm going to get it. He has wrapped himself up, neck and navel, to an unscrupulous political minority. I am preparing a full exposure. (*He flourishes a document.*) On this piece o' paper I've got half the facts I'm seeking. When the list is complete, I shall broadcast it out before the voters o' this borough! They'll know what to do! . . . *And* he won't get his first-class travelling expenses neither, I can tell you.

BOOCOCK. I, er, I hope, gentlemen, you won't try and build this up into too much of a sensation . . . er . . . thank you very much . . .

Exeunt all save JOURNALISTS.

JOURNALISTS. Thank you, Mr Mayor.

1ST JOURNALIST. Right. Number one demonstration of prejudice and bias. Now for number two.

2ND JOURNALIST. Boots polished, trousers pressed, anybody need a haircut ? Very good. Shall we take our places ?

They move round the stage

SCENE THREE

The Police headquarters.

JOURNALISTS *still on stage. Enter* FENG, WIPER *and a* PC.

FENG. Gentlemen, I am exceedingly sorry that Alderman Butterthwaite has chosen to publish these allegations. There is, of course, *no* political influence behind the conduct of the police. What else do you expect me to say ?

2ND JOURNALIST. Would you be willing to talk matters over with His Worship the Mayor, if . . .

FENG. His Worship the Mayor has apparently taken as gospel everything Alderman Butterthwaite has seen fit to tell him! So what is there left to talk about, pray ? Personally I would welcome an inquiry. An independent inquiry, conducted by the Home Office. And none other! That is all. I thank you. Good morning.

JOURNALISTS. Good morning, Colonel. Thank you very much . . .

The PC *shows them out and then stands well aside.*

FENG. Now tell me, Superintendent. What am I to think ?

Both you and Sir Harold have given me the benefit of your no doubt independent analyses of this miserable affair, and certainly the public attitude of our Socialist friends would appear to bear you out. But supposing behind their demagogic antics there were in fact some truth? This sergeant you sent round to the club . . . what's his name? Lumber?

WIPER. Yessir. Sarnt Lumber.

FENG. What's his record?

WIPER. An exceedingly good one, sir. I would personally stand very fast indeed behind Sergeant Lumber . . . We could, of course, suspend him until the matter has been cleared up?

FENG. No. They would tell us, would they not, that there is no smoke without fire. But you will investigate, Superintendent, both deeply and confidentially, and I shall be investigating your investigation, and I shall be investigating *you*, sir.

WIPER. Oh . . . in that case, Colonel Feng, I must ask you to accept my resignation.

FENG. No. If you have done your duty, you will indeed feel your honour impugned. But it is not only *your* honour, it is the honour of the entire force, it is *my* honour, sir, *mine*, that is being dragged like a dead dog through the egalitarian garbage of these streets!

WIPER. You're quite right, sir, quite right. I withdraw my resignation.

FENG. I am glad to find your reaction so extremely correct . . . Now above all, Superintendent, let us not get rattled. Cool nerves, keen brains, no statements to the Press. We will soon defeat these unworthy attempts. They are a symptom of the age, I have met them before. It is not difficult to prevail against them. I look forward to your report.

Exit WIPER. PC *helps* FENG *into coat and hat and umbrella and goes.*

I am a man under authority. Having soldiers under me, or at least constables, and I say to this man 'go' and he goeth, and

to another 'come' and he cometh, and to my servant 'do this'
and he doeth it . . .
Not difficult to prevail but difficult indeed
To live and hold that prevalence, yet live
A social and communicating creature.
The law by nature is civilian,
But it can only work through mode of warfare.
So, we, like soldiers through the English streets,
They fear us while they look to us for strength.
The violence of authority seems to grow
In face of growing violence of crime,
Wrying the neck of our disturbed profession.
They call me Colonel, but by courtesy,
I command and serve, and which is which ? Who knows ?
I tell you, I do not. We used to wear
Top hats and sober clothes like sober tradesmen
But where top hats were worn the heads were broke,
So, military helmets. And the tunics,
Once frock-coats, breed badges and bright buttons,
Confirming in their cut to use of war.
We are not armed. I fear we shall be soon.
I hope we must be. There are too many dead.
Yet then how can we say we only serve
Civilian purposes ? The pay is low
So nobody will join. Then raise the pay
And bad recruits will join for money only ?
I have no hope and therefore walk alone :
Only alone can I know I am right.

SCENE FOUR

A public park.

FENG, *on stage still, walks about in meditation, then sits down*
wearily on a seat, which a PARK ATTENDANT *brings him.*

WELLESLEY *comes in, depressed. She walks about, too, then sits down as well and pays the* ATTENDANT *for her seat.*

FENG. Er h'm . . . Miss Blomax, is it not?

WELLESLEY. H'm? . . . Oh yes. Good morning.

FENG. I – er – I think we have had the pleasure. Er – Feng – how do you do?

WELLESLEY. We met at the Sweetmans'.

FENG. We did. At the Sweetmans'.

WELLESLEY. Are you all by yourself, then – or—?

FENG. Oh, yes: quite as usual, all by myself. A short turn in the park during the luncheon-break. Companions, of course, invidious, to a man in my position. As it were, the ship's captain.

WELLESLEY. Ship's—?

FENG. Oh yes. Private quarters under the quarter-deck and so forth: unwise to be too general, a necessary loneliness, I am sure you will understand me, you being also known in these curious parts as an enemy alien, are you not, Miss Blomax?

WELLESLEY. A what?

FENG. I mean, from the South?

WELLESLEY. Oh no, I live in Westmorland.

FENG. Oh yes. Of course. The forests . . . Your father is a native here?

WELLESLEY. I think he was born in Twickenham.

FENG. Ah? Ah yes, the South . . .

> *They sit for a while.* FENG *acknowledges the salute of a passing* PC.

You made, I recollect, at Sir Harold's table, a few remarks about the government of the town, which struck me at the time as, er – somewhat penetrating, Miss Blomax. You will no doubt forgive me if I appeared to have dismissed them. I have now, however, reason to believe you may have spoken more shrewdly than you realized.

WELLESLEY. Oh, I realized very well. You can tell all you

want to know about the climate of the town by the arrangement and the trimming of the trees in this park.

FENG. Ah yes, the trees. I quite agree with you. Barbarous. No notion how to plant. No notions at all. Borough engineering. A tee-square and a compass and lop off every branch that refuses to conform. Barbarous!

WELLESLEY. I wouldn't have thought you'd have had that much sympathy for a nonconformist tree.

FENG. Trees are not people. They are a gentle entertainment provided by our Creator for ourselves and for Himself. It is churlish to abuse them. We must educate our society and prevent such abuse.

WELLESLEY. Educate? . . . Oh, I'm so glad I didn't go to school here. I've got my father to thank for that if for nothing else. The day that you leave school here you're expected to reach the age of forty in about three hours and that's all. If you won't do it, you know what you get? Hump of the old shoulders and the old grunt comes out at you!

> Too young, too tall, and your eyes too bright,
> You look too near and you look too hard,
> You dream too deep in the deep of the night,
> And you walk too long in my backyard.
> You stand and ask for your white bread
> And you stand and you ask for your brown,
> But what you will get is a good horse whip
> To drive you out of town.

How old are you, as a matter of interest?

FENG. Oh? Oh, sufficiently old. No longer irresponsible. Rigid, you might say. Hardened arteries, young lady, unsympathetic and crumbling. Hardness, however, is nothing if not necessary. It derives from my post and my years in the Colonial Service and the necessity therein for unwavering powers of decision. And so I *have* decided. Quite suddenly. Unexpectedly. I am, alone, not sufficient, in fact I am bewildered. Particularly now, surrounded as I am by a confusion of

democracy and alien loyalties, for support I turn – where?
Of necessity to another alien. I would like you to become my
wife . . . Or do you not perhaps share my belief in the
similarity of our predicaments? I have within me – I mean as
a man, not a policeman – an extraordinary humanity, of
necessity concealed. Improbable longings, attempts at self-
betrayal, I think I can crush them, by this improbable
method. I would be glad of your opinion.

WELLESLEY. Oh dear . . . Oh no . . . I don't think it's very
likely. I mean, I don't think –

FENG. Perhaps it is not. It would have been easier for me to
have forgotten my impulse and to have continued our conversation upon a more usual subject. As it might be, the
trees. Perhaps it is not too late for me yet to forget it . . . or,
I observe you are a pedestrian. I always prefer to talk to
pedestrians, at least of our milieu . . . They are the less
likely – you see – to bear a grudge against my occupation . . .
but I have a car around the corner. Do you think I could possibly offer you a lift anywhere?

WELLESLEY. I was just sitting in the park. There is nowhere I
want to go to, really . . .

FENG. Yes. By all means. I wish I could sit with you further.
But duty, alas . . . Good day to you, Miss Blomax. I, er, I
would look forward very much to meeting you again, some
time? . . . Good day . . .

Exit FENG.
She sits for a while, then YOUNG SWEETMAN *enters.*

YOUNG SWEETMAN. Wellesley . . . hello . . . Wellesley.

WELLESLEY. . . . I suppose you've come to tell me that they
have told you that you must never see me again?

YOUNG SWEETMAN. Well, as a matter of fact . . .

WELLESLEY. All the old grey heads are breaking one another's
blood out, because of who saw what of what girl below the
waist, when we all know very well they would *all* love to see

it. And why shouldn't they? It's a free country. Have you
seen it?

YOUNG SWEETMAN. What?

WELLESLEY. At the Copacabana, Maurice. Have you seen it?

YOUNG SWEETMAN. As a matter of fact, yes.

WELLESLEY. And who tells the truth about it? You tell me
that, the Reds or the Fascists?

YOUNG SWEETMAN. Neither, of course.

WELLESLEY. So there you are. Yet those are the people who
claim they can regulate your life and my life, and make our
unwavering decisions. Not for what they think of us, but for
what they think of each other. We have no obligation to
them. Only to ourselves; we ought to fight for what we want.
What do *you* want, Maurice?

YOUNG SWEETMAN. You.

WELLESLEY. Do you? – I wish I knew what *I* did . . . I have
a father and he calls himself a stumbling-block. If only there
was someone to show me the way to turn him into a stepping-
stone . . .

> *She goes out.* YOUNG SWEETMAN *follows after her calling
> 'Wellesley . . . Wellesley . . .'*
> *Enter* BLOMAX *with a brown paper parcel.*

BLOMAX. Oh dear, oh dear . . . Beverley Races, what a performance! Ben Jonson's Delight was pulled by his jock and I
lost a cool fifty. What's more, I wasn't warned. I don't know
why the stewards don't enforce these things better. Something's gone very queer with my sources of advance information. And not only at Beverley. What have I come back to!
Well, you've seen it more than I have. *I* don't know where
it's going to conclude . . . I suppose it would be strategical
to have a word with Gloria? I last left her at Doncaster, very
astonished. On such a beautiful evening – now that club of
hers is apparently closed – she will no doubt be found supine
in her back garden, enjoying a drink of tea . . .

SCENE FIVE

The back garden of GLORIA'S *house.*

BLOMAX *remains on stage.* GLORIA *and* WIPER *enter for sun-bathing in the garden with a crate of beer.* WIPER *is playing an accordion. They do not notice* BLOMAX *at first.*

BLOMAX. Oh well, more or less . . . Somebody's sense of crisis isn't very highly developed. I suppose you could call it the good old British phlegm . . .

WIPER (*singing*).

>   The lady's walls are large and high
>   The lady's grass is green and dry
>   The lady herself is green and blooming
>   And big fat Alfred, he's consuming . . .

Here, have another . . . (*He passes a bottle.*)

GLORIA (*to* WIPER). I hope you know what you're doing, sprawling here in broad daylight. I don't call it safe.

WIPER. Of course it's bloody safe. I came in the back gate, I go out the ditto, and we're not overlooked . . .

BLOMAX. Cock-a-doodle-doo . . .

They both leap up in alarm.

WIPER. Good God, how did *you* get in here?

BLOMAX. I carry a key in my little fob pocket.

WIPER. Oh you do, do you? And might I ask you why?

BLOMAX. And might I ask *you* why you've abandoned Mrs Wiper in such very hot weather with all the washing-up in a stuffy little kitchen?

WIPER. Leave my wife out of it.

BLOMAX. All right then, you leave *mine*.

WIPER. What? What's that!

He whips round on GLORIA, *who nods her head.*

GLORIA. Doncaster Registry Office. Monday morning. On his way to the races. It seemed the safest notion. But that gives you no cause to come barging in here as if you owned the bloody place . . .

BLOMAX. Now then, my dear, don't let's get edgy. A woman in your condition . . .

WIPER. But why didn't you tell me?

GLORIA. I didn't want to spoil things.

WIPER. You didn't want to spoil things . . . !

Knocking on the garden gate.

GLORIA. Oh my Lord, who's that! (*She calls out.*) No thank you, not today; I never buy at the gate!

Knocking continues.

I'd better open, I suppose. Keep out of sight. We don't know *who* it might be.

She hurriedly pulls on a housecoat over her bikini. WIPER *thrusts himself into his trousers and gathers up his shirt, tunic, etc.* BLOMAX *runs into the house.* GLORIA *opens the gate.* LADY SWEETMAN *enters.*

Lady Sweetman! How do you do?

LADY SWEETMAN. I am not very well. I have a migraine head-ache. Do you think I could come in a minute?

GLORIA *has to let her in the gate.*

Sir Harold Sweetman, Sir Harold, I may tell you, Sir Harold is extremely upset.

GLORIA. Aye, I can believe you . . .

WIPER, *who has not quite finished doing up his buttons, is caught.*

LADY SWEETMAN. Superintendent Wiper?

WIPER (*adjusting his buttons*). Good evening, Lady Sweetman.

LADY SWEETMAN. I know what you are here for, Superintendent. I know all about it.

WIPER. You do?

LADY SWEETMAN. And may I say I am appalled. You see, Sir Harold is a sick man. He has a coronary condition. All these cabals, these distasteful intrigues, I may tell you, are killing him. (*She sniffs at her camphor.*)

GLORIA. A very jolly deathbed and all by the look of his complexion.

LADY SWEETMAN. Coronary trouble expresses itself in an unhealthy heightened colour.

GLORIA. Aye . . .

LADY SWEETMAN. However, we have no course but to be practical. I came here to find out what my husband refuses to tell me. How deeply is he involved in this unpleasant affair at the Copacabana?

WIPER. Up to the lug-oyles.

LADY SWEETMAN. Oh . . . He is most confident, you understand, that he will be able to extricate himself, and even, I think, use it to political advantage.

WIPER. I'm delighted to hear that, Lady Sweetman. It really does me good.

LADY SWEETMAN. But is his confidence justified?

WIPER. It all depends on Colonel Feng and how deep he decides to delve. He could burn our bottoms yet, could Colonel Feng.

GLORIA. Never mind about Feng. What about Butterthwaite?

LADY SWEETMAN. Has he made a definite accusation?

GLORIA. No, but he soon will.

LADY SWEETMAN. And if so, can he prove it?

GLORIA. That chap can prove anything if he's left alone with it long enough. It's up to us to get in first and on a field of our own choosing. Do him down through summat else.

LADY SWEETMAN. Not politics. It mustn't be politics. Think of my husband's heart.

GLORIA. All right then. We'll keep it personal. But what?

LADY SWEETMAN. I think we should consider Mr Butter-thwaite's character. Such outrageous vulgarity must be there for a purpose, you know. Nobody could behave like that naturally.

WIPER. Oh, I don't know, Lady Sweetman. An astonishing great deal comes very naturally to some of us. (*He offers her a beer.*) Here – have a wet. The old family firm, you know.

LADY SWEETMAN. No, thank you . . . No, it is deliberate. He is concealing a social weakness. Of course, he is bound to feel inferior in many respects.

GLORIA. I can tell you one respect where he not only *feels* but he very definitely *is*.

LADY SWEETMAN. Oh. And what is that?

GLORIA. The gee-gees.

LADY SWEETMAN. The—

WIPER. She's not wrong, you know, she's right. If he tried to fix the ballot boxes as crafty as he fixes the Tote, there'd be no Labour Party left.

LADY SWEETMAN. Tote, Superintendent? Gee-gees? I don't quite . . .

GLORIA. The races, Lady Sweetman. He loses his bets.

LADY SWEETMAN. Ah . . . Oh well, that makes it much easier. We must expose him, of course.

WIPER. How? He never bounced any cheques so far as I know . . .

GLORIA. He never *used* any cheques. But there must be a couple o' hundred quid at least queuing up in his I O U's.

LADY SWEETMAN. You see? It's all quite easy. We must find out who his creditors are and, er, assemble what my husband calls a Pressure Group. Sir Harold will be so grateful, you know. He never will believe that we women have a place in public life, but—

GLORIA. It's assembled already, the Pressure Group. It con-sists of one creditor only and his name is Wellington Blomax.

LADY SWEETMAN. Oh – Dr Blomax!

GLORIA. You know him? Well, he's just acquired a highly intelligent new wife.

LADY SWEETMAN. Oh, I'm so glad. I've always said that poor child of his needs a properly organized home, and I don't think she's been getting it.

GLORIA. No . . .

LADY SWEETMAN. Well, we must approach Mrs Blomax and make her understand – as I am sure that she will, being a woman – that her husband has a manifest duty to the community—

BLOMAX (*inside*). Wellesley, I'm warning you, you'll not be welcome out there—

GLORIA. Hey up – who's in the house!

Enter WELLESLEY.

WELLESLEY. He's just told me you're his wife!

LADY SWEETMAN. *You* are!

GLORIA. I dare say it does come as a bit of a surprise . . . Lady Sweetman, my – er – my stepdaughter, I suppose . . . It's the first time we've met.

LADY SWEETMAN. How very convenient. So we can keep it all in our own little circle and save so much unpleasantness. Now, Wellesley . . .

GLORIA. Superintendent, it's time you were off. Your recreation's over. Get back to Mrs Wiper.

WIPER. What? Why? Hey—

GLORIA. I don't want you to know too much. You'll only muck it up again if you do. But it is very unwise to fall asleep too soon in the shade of so dangerous an orchard. Keep hold on the fruit-basket – watch out for what drops.

WIPER. What drops? Where?

GLORIA. Butterthwaite. He's ripe enough . . . Go on, get off with you.

WIPER. Oh, oh, very well . . . Good evening, Lady Sweetman.

Exit.

LADY SWEETMAN. Good evening, Superintendent . . . Quite a nice man – when you get to know him better.

GLORIA. Nice? Oh aye . . .

WELLESLEY (*takes beer*). Do you mind, I feel thirsty . . . He left one of his little notes on his surgery door to say where he was for the benefit of his patients. It'd just serve you right to get six kids with measles and a couple of polio subjects interrupting the honeymoon. (*To* LADY SWEETMAN.) I suppose you've come to see my father to complain about me and Maurice and all the rest of that?

LADY SWEETMAN. Complain? Oh my dear child, I'm not going to complain. Do you *want* to marry Maurice? He wants to marry *you*, you know.

WELLESLEY. I have had other offers. I have not yet made a choice. All that I want is my right to do so, unprejudiced, when I want, do you see? I want it and I'll fight for it.

BLOMAX *enters, behind, listening.*

LADY SWEETMAN. Oh, you young people – so noisy about your *rights*. But what about your responsibilities, Wellesley? I don't know whether you will understand this, my dear, because, of course, you're not entirely English, are you? But I am afraid that you yourself must to some extent be held responsible for your father.

WELLESLEY. Responsible? Me? Are you out of your mind?

LADY SWEETMAN. I have always been told he is a very good doctor – at least for his panel patients. But as a professional man, he must know very well he is known by his friends.

WELLESLEY. His friends aren't *my* friends.

LADY SWEETMAN. Yes, my dear, I know. And *you* must make yourself responsible for seeing they are no longer *his*. I am going to be quite strict about this, Wellesley, and I'm going

to apply pressure. He must be made to understand the folly
of his conduct. And then we shall *all* be happy. You will, *and*
Maurice. Yes . . . Good-bye, Mrs er – Blomax, I leave it all
in your hands . . . Oh dear, my poor head . . . In your
hands, Mrs Blomax. I do hope I can trust you . . .

Exit
BLOMAX *comes forward.*

GLORIA. So you overheard us, did you ? . . . Pressure. You'd
do well to prepare yourself.

BLOMAX. I don't know what you are talking about, Wellesley,
my dove. I bought two pair o' kippers. Not much, but they're
protein. You see, I had a bad day.

GLORIA. The news may not have filtered through to you at the
Beverley Grandstand, but Alfred Wiper and your flash companions from the Victoria and Albert have grown somewhat
incompatible.

BLOMAX. Flash companions indeed! They are very old friends
of mine.

GLORIA. That's the trouble. You realize what's happened to
Alfred ? He is lined up with Sweetman. And your daughter,
as it happens, has a taste and fancy also to line up with
Sweetman . . .

WELLESLEY. Wait a minute . . .

GLORIA. You just keep quiet, love. All I want *you* to do is to
stand over there and look pathetic. (*To* BLOMAX *again.*)
You'd be well advised to take example and to line yourself up
likewise. I mean, get rid of Butterthwaite, and join your own
class of people. Don't you want her to stand in the favour of
her chosen new in-laws ? And besides, your own position in
regard to the police isn't all that it might be. Suppose they
were to hear about what you've been prescribing for certain
other of your female patients ?

BLOMAX. An issue of mercy, their condition demanded it . . .

GLORIA. Yes . . .

BLOMAX. Yes . . . of course, I do acknowledge a definite duty towards my neglected little daughter . . . But *I* don't know . . . Charlie Butterthwaite? What do you expect me to *do* about him, Gloria?

GLORIA. Tell him where you stand and tell him who you are? Be decisive. Insult him. Press him for your debts. You'll be done with him *then*. Don't tell me you've got qualms?

WELLESLEY. How can he have qualms? He's an old rotten rascal and he's given me no good ever. I want what I want and I'm going to break his head for it. Are we to have these for supper?

She takes the kippers into the house.

BLOMAX. You'd better go and help her. She'll turn those kippers into charcoal if you give her half a chance.

GLORIA. We want an answer from you before you go to bed.

BLOMAX. Bed?

GLORIA. Aye, bed . . .

> And the shape of your answer
> Will doubtless decide
> Whether that bed
> Will be narrow or wide! – hubby!

She goes into the house.

BLOMAX. Well, whether it's one or whether it's the other, I still seem to have invited into it the east wind and the west and they're scrapping like two catamounts between my skin and my pyjamas . . .

He picks up the empty bottles, pours out the dregs into one bottle, and drinks it.

Fact of the matter is, I *have* been betraying my class. Wellesley *is* entitled to the natural advantages of her place in society, the snooty little bitch. I am, after all, a comfortable man: and

I don't want to be disrupted. When all is said and done, this town is run by an ignorant overweening yobbo: and it's time I stood up firm to him and accepted the responsibilities of my superior education . . . Furthermore, he owes me money.

    He goes into the house

SCENE SIX

A room in the Town Hall.

    Enter BOOCOCK, LEFTWICH *and* HOPEFAST.

HOPEFAST.
> He came and asked for thirty quid,
> I said I hadn't got it.
> I said I wasn't made o' brass,
> He said he bloody knew it.

BOOCOCK.
> I can't imagine Charlie
> Running really short o' money.
> He hasn't said a word to me.

HOPEFAST.
> I think there's summat funny.

LEFTWICH.
> He's lost it on the horses.

    Enter HARDNUTT.

HARDNUTT.
> I think there's summat funny.
> Did you hear Charlie Butterthwaite
> Wor trying to borrow money?

BOOCOCK.
> He never said a word to me.
> I've been often pleased to lend him

      The odd quid here and there,
      I gave it him, he gave it back,
      All fair and no one wondered.

LEFTWICH.

      He's lost it on the horses.

BOOCOCK.

      He can't have done.

HARDNUTT.

      He did.

HOPEFAST.

      He did.

HARDNUTT.

      It sounds to me like balaclava Bugles,
      This day some clown has blundered.

BOOCOCK.

      We all know Charlie Butterthwaite,
      And know him without turpitude,
      Nine times he's held the rank of Mayor,
      And now the peoples' gratitude.
      With all the battles he has fought
      In all his loyal rectitude
      If he should be in trouble
      We should grant him our support.

Enter HICKLETON.

HICKLETON.

      What's up with our old Charlie,
      Asking everyone for money?
      I mean to say he's often short . . .

BOOCOCK.

      We all of us are often short.

HICKLETON.

      He asked me for one hundred quid!
      And coming at a time like this,
      The day we've all but clapped the lid

On Feng and Sweetman and the Tories . . .
I think there's summat funny,
And I hear there's funny stories
Have been spread around about.

HARDNUTT.

His face wor red and white
And his eyes wor poking out.

HICKLETON.

And asking me for five score quid.

HOPEFAST.

He rang me up i' t'midst o' t'night,
First in a chuckle, then in a shout.

HICKLETON.

And then he came to my front door.
I said, o'course, I hadn't got it.

HICKLETON ⎫
HOPEFAST ⎭

I said I wasn't made o'brass.

ALL 3 COUNCILLORS.

He said he bloody knew it!

Enter BUTTERTHWAITE.

BUTTERTHWAITE. Hello! I know. I've got red ears . . . All
right, I don't come twice to a sold-out chip-oyle, t'subject's
done with. Now, Mr Mayor, there's a delegate outside from
the Forces of Reaction. Are you going to talk to him?

BOOCOCK. I am. And this time, Charlie, you keep your oar out.
I am highly concerned for our reputation abroad. Have you
seen the *Yorkshire Post* today?

BUTTERTHWAITE. Aye, it were good reading. I tell you,
they're getting frightened.

BOOCOCK. I don't call it good reading. We're in the London
Telegraph an' all, let alone that two-faced *Herald*. The time
has now come for appropriate negotiations.

BUTTERTHWAITE. Appropriate? All right, but Feng has got to go.

BOOCOCK. Eh dear . . . I don't know . . . Herbert, let him in.

LEFTWICH *ushers in* F. J.

F. J. Good evening, Mr Mayor. May I take it you are speaking for the Labour Party as I in my turn am speaking for the Conservatives?

SWEETMAN *comes in and stands at the back.*

BUTTERTHWAITE (*pointing to* SWEETMAN). I see him, over there!

BOOCOCK. Charlie, do you mind?

F. J. Bearing in mind the unsettling effect of such a dispute and particularly in regard to the criminal element of the town . . .

BOOCOCK. Granted.

F. J. I beg your pardon?

BOOCOCK. Granted.

F. J. Mr Mayor, I beg you, please moderate your attitude. The police should be above party recrimination.

BOOCOCK. Granted.

F. J. Sir Harold is thinking in terms of an independent inquiry. He has authorized me to . . .

BOOCOCK. Alderman Butterthwaite has laid a definite information. It is the duty of the Chief Constable to either prosecute the Copacabana or to give adequate reasons for refusing to prosecute. If he should finally determine to refuse, then I imagine an inquiry would be mandatory. But until then, certainly not.

F. J. But, Mr Mayor . . .

BOOCOCK. And let alone the whole question of corruption in his ranks!

F. J. If you will not agree to a Home Office inquiry, Sir Harold is fully prepared to lay the facts at his disposal in front of the electorate. And they are not entirely synonymous with those presented by Alderman Butterthwaite.

BOOCOCK. Who has presented *no* facts! Sub judice evidence cannot be publicly brought forward.

F. J. Not brought forward. Slid.

BOOCOCK. I beg your pardon?

F. J. Granted. I said 'slid'. Rumours deliberately insinuated. We may be reactionaries, Barney, but we're not complete idiots. There's plenty of personal dirt we can throw into the next election. We don't like it, we've never done it, but if we have to, we will!

BOOCOCK. I'm sure your hearts will bleed.

F. J. Oh, and by the way, the art gallery. You may not believe it, but there are certain people who regard it as important.

BOOCOCK. *I* regard it as important. What the hell are you talking about?

SWEETMAN. It has been shuffled once too often. I am now making it my personal concern.

Exeunt SWEETMAN *and* F. J.

BOOCOCK. Well, you all heard him. An independent inquiry! Now that's a very big concession. I think we ought to take it.

COUNCILLORS *murmur agreement.*

BUTTERTHWAITE. Oh, no, no, no . . . I'm not being fobbed off wi' no cocoa-and-water compromises. I want my gullet stuffed wi' the good fat roast goose to the point of a vomit, *and* I'm getting it an' all.

BOOCOCK. Ah . . . What do you think he meant about the art gallery, Charlie?

BUTTERTHWAITE. The art gallery's been attended to.

BOOCOCK. And after what manner attended to, Charlie?

BUTTERTHWAITE. It's all in the Committee Minutes if you care to look it up. A unanimous decision was taken against any further discussion of the point.

BOOCOCK. Two Conservatives on that Committee. Which way
did they vote?

BUTTERTHWAITE. They were unavoidably absent.

BOOCOCK. Oh, they were, were they? By, Charlie Butterthwaite, if I wor a younger man I'd put my bloody booit into
thee! Who do you think you are, going behind my back like
that!

BUTTERTHWAITE. I'll tell you who I am.

> I'm the King of this Castle, Barney,
> And that by right of conquest,
> Elected for main engagement
> In each and every issue
> Our party has pursued
> Throughout perilous generations.
> I turned tramcars over
> In the turmoil of twenty-six,
> I marched in the hungry mutiny
> From the north to the metropolis,
> I carried the broken banner.
> When hungry bellies bore no bread,
> I dreamed of my dinner
> In the wasted line of dole,
> And by fundamental force of strength
> I fetched my people through it.
> Call it the Red Sea, call it
> The boundaries of Canaan,
> I carried them over,
> My care, my calculation
> Lived as a loyal Englishman
> Through long-suffering and through languishment,
> I chiefly did, and I chiefly deserved.
> Can you deny it?

BOOCOCK. No. Chiefly is true. But party is party. We cannot
call it 'King'.

BUTTERTHWAITE. I spoke by way of metaphor.

BOOCOCK. We cannot call it 'King'.

BUTTERTHWAITE. Ah, Barney, Barney, Barney . . . Constable Leftwich, look at us both! Which one's the King?

LEFTWICH. Neither. I'd say Mrs Boocock.

They all laugh.

BUTTERTHWAITE. How *is* the missus, Barney?

BOOCOCK. Sarah continues robust.

BUTTERTHWAITE (*taking him aside*). And I suppose she still holds the old Boocock cheque-book, eh?

BOOCOCK. Ah . . . I wondered when you were going to pluck up face and come to me about it. How much is the total?

BUTTERTHWAITE. She'd never let you have it.

BOOCOCK. Three figures, they wor telling me . . . I'm afraid that she wouldn't. I'm afraid there's not a chance. Now a tenner or a fiver.

BUTTERTHWAITE. Nay, I'd not take it.

BOOCOCK. All right, I'll not force you . . . It's time we were off home. You can be locking up, Herbert; the office staff will all have gone.

LEFTWICH. Goodnight, Mr Mayor.

BOOCOCK (*turning back on the way out*). Now, Charlie, this inquiry, think it over very careful. I believe we should agree to it . . .

BOOCOCK AND COUNCILLORS. Night, Charlie, night Charlie . . . etc.

Exeunt all save BUTTERTHWAITE *and* LEFTWICH.

BUTTERTHWAITE. Go and lock up. I won't be half an hour. I've got some letters to attend to.

LEFTWICH. I say, Charlie, is it that bad?

BUTTERTHWAITE. There's nowt that bad, Herbert, as can't be made better with a bit o' pride of achievement in some other field. All I want to do is get rid o' Feng. If I can manage

that, I don't give a bastard's egg if I spend the rest o' my life
i' t'workhouse!

LEFTWICH. Well, you were born i' t'bloody place, worn't you?

Exit LEFTWICH.

BUTTERTHWAITE. Wellington! Wellington! You scarlet intes-
tine-rummaging dun, where ha' you got to?

Enter BLOMAX.

BLOMAX. Are you alone yet?
BUTTERTHWAITE. I am.
BLOMAX. Have you got it?
BUTTERTHWAITE. I have not.
BLOMAX. I am sorry to do this, Charlie! I've got to have that
money!
BUTTERTHWAITE. Five hundred bloody nicker . . .
BLOMAX. Charlie, you're a cheat. You're a chiseller. You're
rotten. You are not a loyal friend.
BUTTERTHWAITE. What!
BLOMAX. I mean to quarrel with you, Charlie. I am forced to
cast you off . . .
BUTTERTHWAITE. Wellington . . . if you weren't in bad
trouble, you would never use such words. Come on, lad,
what is it? Are you being blackmailed?
BLOMAX. Oh, Charlie, I am! You see, it's been like this. I'm
going to be frank with you, Charlie. I – I er don't know how
to put it . . . it's a question of – a – question of – all right,
professional reputation. Yes. Now here is the truth! Over-
indulgent prescriptions! Suppose I put it that way? . . . I
only regarded it as an extension of a normal bedside manner.
But it looks like coming up at a coroner's inquest, so I've got
to pay up or hic haec hoc, I'm done!
BUTTERTHWAITE. Are you telling me the truth?
BLOMAX. The absolute and clear-starched verity! I'm always
being half blackmailed, but this time it's dead serious. Oh,

Charlie, I've done you a power of services up and down this town as a general intelligencer, and if ever you've found me of any use at all . . .

BUTTERTHWAITE. It has never been said that Charlie Butterthwaite was the man to watch his mates fall under. Gratitude wi' Charlie for services rendered is the king-post of his rooftree:

> It holds the tiles above his house-place
> The smoke-hole for his fire
> It overhangs his weighty table
> And the bed of his desire!

Wellington, you'll have your money, but out o' *my* bank-balance? Oh dear . . . How are we going to manage?

BLOMAX. I don't know. How are we?

BUTTERTHWAITE. Burgle t'Town Hall.

BLOMAX. It's all right *laughing* . . .

BUTTERTHWAITE. Wellington, I'm not laughing . . . Did I ever tell you I was born in the workhouse? Well I was, and it was horrible. Oh, they've not got me back there yet, not a carrot nor a stick can compel this bloody donkey where he doesn't want to go! (*He sings, with a little dance.*)

> In the workhouse I was born
> On one Christmas day
> Two long ears and four short feet
> And all I ate was hay.
>
> Hay for breakfast, hay for dinner
> Lovely hay for tea,
> I thanked my benefactors thus
> Hee-haw hee-haw *hee!*

Now then, it's none so very difficult. All you need to know is the right key to t'safe. I've got it on me watchchain. We make a quick glance around in the interests of security, good, they've all gone home to their teas, we open it up . . . (*He opens the safe*.) And . . . the Borough Treasurer's petty cash!

(*He sings*.)

> When I was grown as tall as this
> I asked if I might go
> Into the world, the lovely world,
> I saw it through the window!

Aye, and they gave me permission and all:

> Get out, they said, you dirty brute,
> You've grown up quite disgusting.
> The world is welcome to your stink
> And to your horrid lusting.
> I thanked my benefactors thus . . . !

BLOMAX. Charlie, I say, Charlie, is this the real issue? I mean to say, there's no real hurry – it's not really that urgent . . .

BUTTERTHWAITE. Of course it's the real issue, you consequential fathead! There's nigh on a thousand in here. I don't know how many times I've had to tell these skiving clerks this is *not* the Barclays Bank!

BLOMAX. But surely they'll have made a note of the numbers?

BUTTERTHWAITE. Not on your life they haven't! Ho, there's some head going to roll in this office tomorrow morning. (*He is counting out packets of banknotes*.) There's your five hundred. Put it in your pocket! Go on, put it in!

(*He sings*.)

> I thanked my benefactors thus
> Hee-haw hee-haw haw.
> I could not understand, you see,
> Just how it was they thought of me
> Or what it was they saw!

What am I going to do wi' t'rest? I might keep it. But I won't. It'll only draw attention . . . I know . . .

He sings, and as he does so he scatters money about the stage.

> I travelled out into that world
> With never a backward glance,
> The street was full of folk, they said,
> He's got two ears upon his head
> He's got four feet upon his legs
> He's got . . . My God, look what he's got,
> They cried, Get back to France!

I said, what do you mean, France? I've never been to France in my life! I wor born in the workhouse. I never set foot over the doorstone while this morning!

> They cried, Get back to France!

Oh my God, it makes me tired . . .

> I could not think what I had done
> That I was so derided
> For Nature gives no donkey less
> Than what I was provided.

You see what I'm doing? We scatter it around, thereby indicating a similitude of ludicrous panic . . . as though disturbed in the act we have fled from the scene in terrified disorder.

> I said – hee-haw – you're very rude
> I do the best I can.
> You couldn't treat me worse, I said,
> If I was a human man!

(*He begins wiping fingerprints away.*) And the minute I said that they all fled away. Not a soul in sight in the whole of that long city . . . starved and hungry, there I stood, Wellington. Ooer, and a rumble-oh in my poor thin belly. All the pubs were shut, aye, and the chip-oyles an' all . . . I walked along slowly by a pawnbroker's window, and as it chanced, I saw my reflection in a gilt-framed ormulo mirror . . .

> O what a shock, I nearly died,
> I saw my ears as small as these,
> Two feet, two hands, a pair of knees,
> My eyeballs jumped from side to side,
> I jumped right round, I bawled out loud,
> You lousy liars, I've found you out!
> I know now why you're fleeing . . .
> I am no donkey, never was,
> I'm a naked human being!

You know, after that, it was easy . . . all I had to do was to buy a suit of clothes . . . they came back, they came back, me boy, and there I prospered, there I grew . . . and you look at me now!

BLOMAX. But how are we going to cover all this up?

BUTTERTHWAITE. Do you mean to tell me you haven't been listening to a word I was singing. I have just given you my entire and lamentable autobiography and all you can say is 'How do we cover it up!' . . . All right then, I'll tell you. It is now eight o'clock as near as makes no difference, and by reason of the inclemency of the weather, it is all but dark outside. I am going to proceed home at a normal pace. On entering my garden gate at approximately eight-twenty-five, I am going to be struck on the head by a blunt instrument, wielded by an unknown criminal, who then secures my bunch of keys, leaps into his motor-car, and drives to the Town Hall. He gains entry through a side door, passes through the administrative offices, and opens the safe. On his departure, he leaves the keys i' t'lock-oyle.

BLOMAX. What about the night-watchman?

BUTTERTHWAITE. Do you mean Herbert Leftwich? We gave him the telly in his room six months ago, and he never stirs

out of it while eleven o'clock at earliest . . . Now I'll tell you
your part! You go straight off home, too. And you'll wait
beside your blower till about a quarter-to-nine when my
landlady (or concubine or whatever you call her) rings you
up with an urgent call for assistance. On arrival, you examine
my person, and discern a serious contusion on the top of me
nut. All right, I'll have to provide one. But I don't want to
kill meself. I rely on your diagnosis to make it appear
sufficiently brutal. And don't you turn up with all that hot
paper stuck inside your wallet. Take it out and bury it. And
any rate, don't spend it all at once. But you don't want to
spend it, you're being blackmailed – my God, they could
trace it back to you if you hand it all over in one lump to some
villain.

BLOMAX. I think I could hold out on him for a few days longer,
but—

BUTTERTHWAITE. I think you'd better had. Our job's to fox
the police, not to assist them . . . Fox the police. By God, it
will fox 'em and all. Feng – we've got him diddled! Corruption they can live with, but incompetence – ho ho! Leftwich
will have bolted the front door by now. You go out the side
way, and see you leave it open. I'm going down by Leftwich's
office to establish my time of departure. He'll let me out the
main door and return straightaway to warming his old frus-
trations in front o' the juke-box jury . . . So there we are, get
home with you! And no bloody dawdling, Wellington, or I
promise you I'll twist your windpipe out!

Exeunt.

After a pause, enter LEFTWICH. *He is on his rounds, with a
torch. He sees a banknote on the stage, picks it up with a
'Tut-tut', sees another, picks it up, sees another, and so on,
casually, until he is led by his paper-chase up to the unlocked
safe. He puts the money in, and turns away.*

LEFTWICH. I never knew a more careless lot in all my born

days. The place could have been robbed ten times over. (*Double-take. He rushes back to the safe, opens it, looks in, shuts it, and turns wildly round.*) Hey! Stop thief!

> LEFTWICH *rushes to the side of the stage and presses a button. Alarm bells ring, all round the theatre.*
> *Police cars, gongs and engines heard. Uniformed* PCS *run in, look at the safe, run out again, run in again, take up positions.*
>
> LUMBER *and* WIPER, *in plain clothes, run in. Fingerprint man and police photographer set about their work.* LEFT-WICH, *hurriedly replacing the money on the stage where he has found it, avoids being seen by the others, and succeeds in pocketing at least one banknote.* BOOCOCK *comes in, registers horror, collides with* WIPER *on the staircase: general confusion.* JOURNALISTS *come in with flash cameras. They take a series of photographs, illustrating:*

(1) WIPER *and* LUMBER *examining evidence.*
(2) BOOCOCK *ditto.*
(3) WIPER *and* LUMBER *taking statement from* LEFT-WICH.
(4) BOOCOCK *taking statement from* LEFTWICH.
(5) WIPER *and* LUMBER *taking statement from* BOOCOCK.
(6) WIPER, LUMBER, BOOCOCK *and* LEFTWICH *taking statements from four* LABOUR COUNCILLORS, *who enter in disarray.*
(7) SWEETMAN *and* F. J. *examining evidence on their entry.*
(8) *The entry of* FENG.

> FENG, *entered last, quickly examines the situation, while everyone else stands back.*

FENG (*to* WIPER, *confidentially*). Probably an inside job, Superintendent. But difficult to establish, I dare say. However, carry on.

Exeunt.

Act Three

SCENE ONE

A tea garden in the park.

Enter BLOMAX *carrying a folded newspaper.*

BLOMAX. I never thought it would work. I let myself be
hypnotized by the magic of his personality . . . him and his
contusion . . . sufficiently brutal . . . *my* diagnosis . . . It
wouldn't have knocked out a three-days-old baby, what I
found on his top! And they're playing cat-and-mouse with
me now . . . for over a week it's been going on!

A plain-clothes PC *enters, reading a newspaper.*

That's a great big purring tom over there, with official-issue
boots on, and he's looking at me through a little hole in the
fold of his *Sheffield Star*. Of course, I can do the same. (*He
opens his paper and makes a hole in it with his finger, through
which he watches the* CONSTABLE.) But where does it get
me? I think I'll have a cup o' tea. There's surely no danger
in that?

> *A* PARK ATTENDANT *arranges tables and a* WAITRESS
> *lays them.*
> BLOMAX *sits down at a table which is laid ready, pours him-
> self a large cup of tea and swallows it noisily. Takes aspirins.
> The* PC *also sits down at an opposite table and continues
> watching from behind his paper.*
> *A man who has sat at a table at the rear of the stage turns
> round and is seen to be* FENG. *Noticing* BLOMAX, *he half
> gets up, indecisively.* BLOMAX *recognizes him and chokes
> into his tea-cup.*

Oh . . . it's got extremely stuffy sitting down all of a sudden

. . . I think I'll take a turn in the park . . . (*To the* WAIT-RESS.) Don't bother with the change, miss. You can buy yourself a . . . a knick-knack! (*He gives her a pound note and hurries out.*)

The PC *gets up to follow, but is intercepted by* FENG.

FENG. What was he doing here?

PC. Third teaplace he's visited since dinnertime, sir. A large pot o' tea and a couple of aspirins in each one. I fancy he's getting nervous.

FENG. So I observe. A change of tactics, Constable. Go after him now and take him down to the station. Tell the Super-intendent to see if he can persuade him to reconsider his original statement. I think he might be ready to.

PC. Very good, sir . . . (*To the* WAITRESS.) I've left it on the table. (*Exit* PC.)

The WAITRESS *approaches* FENG.

WAITRESS. The usual, sir?

FENG. If you please. A variety of cakes. I thank you . . . Ah . . .

WELLESLEY *enters.* FENG *holds a chair back and she sits down with him.*

Miss Blomax . . . I'm so glad you could come. I have ordered the tea . . . I do not think, Miss Blomax, that you ought to have come . . . I do not think I should have asked you.

WELLESLEY. Go on, tell me why.

FENG. It is not possible.

WELLESLEY. Of course it is . . . I'm going to have one of these with the toothpaste in. (*She takes an éclair.*) Why don't you have one yourself? And drive off the black bull from the top of your tongue.

FENG.

> It is not possible that I should tell you why.
>
> I have not known you very long.
>
> For right or wrong
>
> Except when authorized for formal public utterance
>
> I must endure perpetual public silence.
>
> And so, for private purposes, I find
>
> My words are of necessity muted.
>
> You have not seemed to mind.
>
> You have drunk tea,
>
> Eaten cakes and toasted bread
>
> And jam, and you yourself have talked to me
>
> And I have been transported.
>
> Did you know it ?

WELLESLEY. Oh yes, I knew it.

FENG. But did you share it ? . . . No.

WELLESLEY. It's not my job to share it. It's your job to be courageous, I suppose, and nasty when you have to . . . Sometimes you can be quite gentle, and, of course, you're sentimental . . . But I don't approve of you, you know. I think I should make that clear because you seem to be working up to a renewal of your proposal.

FENG.

> No! It is not so. It cannot be.
>
> It is not possible. I am destroyed in you.
>
> Do you not see,
>
> By my official bond I am destroyed
>
> And you yourself in me.
>
> I cannot talk or think proposals, either way or none.
>
> Not now. I cannot recognize your company. Not now!
>
> Although in one sense, I suppose, the damage has been done.

WELLESLEY. Because of my father.

FENG. I did not say so.

WELLESLEY. You don't believe what he told you about the attack on the Alderman. If you want to marry me, you're in a difficult position . . . I don't know what to say. I don't want my father to go to prison. I don't want to make things any worse for you . . . you're the only one of the old grey heads I have any respect for. I don't want to hurt you, though I don't care if I *have* to . . . And after a fashion I'm engaged to Maurice Sweetman, and I don't really know whether I like him at all. In a way I'd prefer you. You *are* some sort of *man*.

FENG. Do you mean that?

WELLESLEY. Why not? But I mean it, *provided* . . . I wish you would change your job. Or at least become a bit human at it and leave my father alone.

FENG. I can't hear what you say . . .

WELLESLEY. I said, leave him alone. He's a damned twisting idiot, but he never did serious hurt.

FENG. No, no, I can't hear! Please leave me alone! . . . Or rather, I'll leave you . . . We might be seen together, we *have* been seen together, *heard* together, look! There is the waitress! (*He shoves some coins on the table.*) Here you are. See. It should include the tea, all the cakes I dare say; you want to eat them, in *my* mouth they are sawdust . . .

WELLESLEY *goes. He tries in vain to stop her.*

No, don't you go . . . It is *I* that should be leaving *you*. (*He collides with the* WAITRESS.)

WAITRESS. How many cakes did you have, sir?

FENG. Cakes? Have? What . . . ?

Enter BOOCOCK.

BOOCOCK. I've been seeking you all afternoon. You may not care for what I stand for, but I *am* Chief Magistrate and I'd say it was up to you to show yourself available for once!

FENG. Mr Mayor, I . . .

BOOCOCK. Five hundred pound and upward burgled out o' my Town Hall, near fifteen days gone by and who's arrested? No one! There are professional thieves living in this town;

they keep their wives and families by it; it's your job to know
their names. All right then, bring 'em in!

FENG. Bring in *whom*, sir?

BOOCOCK. The lot in, one by one, till you find out the man!
Instead o' which to choose to doubt the open word of an alderman and a doctor, honest and reputed, doubt their word and
watch their houses, tread upon their heels i' t'street . . .

FENG. Mr Mayor, I cannot hear you!

Enter LABOUR COUNCILLORS.

HOPEFAST. Call your traps off Charlie Butterthwaite, Feng.

HICKLETON. Call 'em off. We want your resignation.

HARDNUTT. We want your resignation!

BOOCOCK. My mind is changed toward you, you've now gone
over t'mark.

BOOCOCK AND COUNCILLORS. We want your resignation!

WAITRESS. Order your teas or else get out. We don't have
brawling here. Do you want me to call the police!

FENG. I told you, sir, I cannot hear one word that you have
said to me!

Exit FENG.

BOOCOCK. There is no further question of reproachment or
conciliation. This is deadlock.

HOPEFAST. Done.

HICKLETON. And capped.

HARDNUTT. And outright ended.

Exeunt

SCENE TWO

The Police headquarters.

PCS *in outer office, ignoring* BUTTERTHWAITE, *who is walking
about with a bandage round his head. He is unshaven and appears
to have taken few pains about the order of his clothes.*

BUTTERTHWAITE (*to the audience*). Will you all take note of what I am about to say. I have been called to this police station by Superintendent Wiper. I have been waiting here for five or six hours, and not one o' these incontinent coppers has taken a blind bit o' notice!

> WIPER *enters his inner office from within. He holds a type-script.*

WIPER. Sarnt Lumber!
LUMBER (*off*). Sir?
WIPER. Time?
LUMBER. Half-twelve, sir. All fixed.

> LUMBER *enters the outer office.* WIPER *comes through to it also.*

WIPER. Afternoon, Alderman. How's the head?
BUTTERTHWAITE. Aches.
WIPER. Oh, dear me. Now to go through your statement just once again, if you don't mind the trouble . . . just a few points . . . (*Refers to typescript.*) On passing through your garden gate, two masked figures rose from behind the privet hedge, one at either gatepost, you were stood betwixt 'em . . . so?

> *He and* LUMBER *at either side of* BUTTERTHWAITE.

Which one hit you?
BUTTERTHWAITE. You did!
WIPER. Sure? It couldn't have been the sergeant?
BUTTERTHWAITE. It could not.
WIPER. But here's the contusion.
BUTTERTHWAITE. Ow, don't touch that bandage!
WIPER. We've had ballistics research in on this. No conceivable injury could from this angle cause even the most temporary failure of the faculties.

BUTTERTHWAITE. You can't catch me. *I've* read me Sexton Blake. I was turned the other way. (*He turns round.*)

WIPER. Are you in the habit, Alderman, of entering your garden backwards?

BUTTERTHWAITE. In the moment of alarm I instinctively swung round to face the open street. What's wrong wi' that?

WIPER. Aha, we're there before you. We photographed your footprints. Quite right, you *were* turned round. Now then, which one hit you?

He and LUMBER *change places.*

BUTTERTHWAITE. You did, you!

WIPER. Me?

BUTTERTHWAITE. No, not you, you booby! *Him.*

WIPER. I see. And from the rear. Now ballistics research has conclusively established . . .

BUTTERTHWAITE. Spare me the Jack Hawkins, will you! The fact remains that I got coshed and here's the wound to prove it. Now get around that if you can.

WIPER. We've got.

BUTTERTHWAITE. You've what?

WIPER. Constable, let's be having him!

Two PCs *bring in* BLOMAX, *rather the worse for wear and holding a mug of tea.*

BUTTERTHWAITE. Wellington! Have they been roughing you up? Oh . . .

WIPER. Dr Blomax, your original statement diagnosing concussion and lesions of the brain has not been borne out by further medical opinion. Do you wish to modify that statement?

LUMBER (*taking a typescript from a* PC). He does, sir.

WIPER. Let's hear it.

BUTTERTHWAITE (*as* LUMBER *is about to read*). I want to telephone my solicitor.

WIPER. All in good time.

BLOMAX. Hey, so do I.

WIPER. If you're going Queen's evidence you don't require a solicitor.

BLOMAX. Oh, Charlie, it's not my fault – they've had me in here all night; I wasn't able to withstand them!

BUTTERTHWAITE. I don't suppose you were. As I have frequently had cause to preach, you can't by individuality hold up props against the overtippling world. By solid class defence and action of the mass alone can we hew out and line with timbered strength a gallery of self-respect beneath the faulted rock above the subsidence of water! Alfred ·Wiper, you watch out. I bear a name that still commands proud worship in these parts!

Enter FENG, *into the outer office.*

FENG. Has the Doctor reconsidered his testimony?

WIPER. He has, sir. Here we are.

FENG *goes into the inner office and* WIPER *follows with* BLOMAX's *statement.*

FENG. I see. It is unusable, I'm afraid.

WIPER. But, sir . . .

FENG. There are reasons, Superintendent, relating to my personal honour, names which might be coupled. I cannot permit this particular man to have the advantage of Queen's evidence. He must stand his trial with the other.

WIPER. We can't do that! He's submitted this voluntarily – we've no choice but to take it. It'll look very queer indeed if—

FENG. Queer?

WIPER. I mean to say, sir, your personal honour . . . Well, folk are going to wonder if it hasn't already become a bit bent.

FENG. That's quite enough of that. You must find out your

own evidence by correct detective measures. I have no more to say.

FENG *goes out through the inner door.* WIPER *returns to the outer office.*

WIPER. Sarnt Lumber, a change of tactic. There is more hard work entailed than we in our innocence had imagined. So send the gentlemen home.

He goes back through the inner office and exits that way.

LUMBER. All right. You heard him. Go home.

BLOMAX. Oh, my dearie me, what an amazing metamorphosis . . . (*He scurries out.*)

BUTTERTHWAITE. Well, well, well, Sergeant. Are you sure it's worth the effort ?

LUMBER. The results of human striving are very rarely worth the effort. For instance, did you hear that after all your worthy struggle the Copacabana Club has closed its doors for the last time, only to re-open on the first day of May as the 'Sweetman Memorial Art Gallery' ? What about that for the artistic interests of the town ?

BUTTERTHWAITE. Why warn't I informed !

LUMBER. You *have* been informed.

BUTTERTHWAITE. In a very irregular manner . . . So he did own that joint all the bloody while, did he ?

LUMBER. I wouldn't know. According to the story, he acquired it last week. *I* wouldn't care to come up with a contradiction. And I don't suppose *you* would . . . under the circumstances.

BUTTERTHWAITE. Get out o' my road !

Exit BUTTERTHWAITE.

LUMBER (*calls after him*). Alderman, be careful, we're not done wi' you yet!

Exeunt

SCENE THREE

The Victoria and Albert.

> *Enter* LABOUR COUNCILLORS, *a few* DRINKERS, LAND-
> LORD *behind bar.*

> *The* COUNCILLORS *sit down at a table.*

HICKLETON. Why hasn't Feng resigned? There's been a
formal council vote of no confidence and yet he's still here!

HOPEFAST. The last I heard o' Charlie, they pulled him in this
morning afore he'd even had his breakfast.

A DRINKER (*sings.*)
O where are the people for to give their voice to glory?
They stand before the altar on the elbow of the Tory . . . !

> *Other* DRINKERS *join in the song and repeat it.*

HARDNUTT. If we can't be private we can take our money else-
where!

LANDLORD (*hurrying over to them*). I'll sort it out . . . (*To the*
DRINKERS.) Now come on, gents, have some decency while
a funeral's in progress!

> *He puts a screen round their table which conceals them from
> the rest of the room.*

But they're not wrong, you know, they're right. There's been
a definite trend in the general talk. (*He goes back to the bar.*)

HOPEFAST. When all is said and done, the image of our party
must not be distorted.

> MRS BOOCOCK *comes in and joins them behind the screen.*

MRS BOOCOCK. Have any o' you seen Barney?

COUNCILLORS. Why, Sarah, sit down, have a chair, love, it's a
surprise to see you here. What are you drinking, etc . . .

MRS BOOCOCK. That doctor's gone Queen's evidence. Start

with the Ways and Means Committee. Have we a quorum?

HARDNUTT. We have.

MRS BOOCOCK. We've not got time to waste. Come on . . .
Councillor Hopefast i' t'chair, Councillor Hardnutt and
Hickleton present in Committee, Mayoress Mrs Boocock as
deputy secretary.

HOPEFAST. I declare the Committee in session.

HARDNUTT. Minutes of the previous meeting regarded as
read . . . Come on . . . Come on . . .

HICKLETON. Seconded.

HOPEFAST. Passed. Motion before the Committee, temporary
absence of Alderman Butterthwaite necessitates reconstruc-
tion of Committee. Who's to replace him?

HICKLETON. I move that Councillor Hathersage be deputed
to do so.

HARDNUTT. Seconded.

HOPEFAST. Passed . . . Now then, Borough Education. I
declare the Committee in session, have we a quorum?

MRS BOOCOCK. I'm in on this one.

HOPEFAST. Councillor Hickleton deputy secretary, change
about places . . . Councillor Hardnutt i' t'chair . . .

HARDNUTT. Minutes of previous meeting . . .

ALL. Etcetera etcetera . . .

HARDNUTT. Motion before . . . etcetera etcetera . . . Who's
to replace him?

MRS BOOCOCK. I move that Councillor Hartwright be deputed
to do so.

HARDNUTT. Seconded. Passed . . . Parks Playgrounds and
Public Baths Committee.

HICKLETON. Councillor Hickleton i' t'chair, Mayoress Mrs
Boocock again deputy secretary.

ALL. Etcetera etcetera . . .

HARDNUTT. Who's to replace him?

HOPEFAST. I move that Councillor Hampole . . .

ALL. Seconded, passed!

HOPEFAST. Any more for any more, we've got no time to waste!

BOOCOCK comes in and joins them. He carries a letter.

MRS BOOCOCK. Barney, where have you been?

BOOCOCK. What are you doing here?

MRS BOOCOCK. I'm having a drink.

BOOCOCK. That's most unwonted, ent it? . . . The Home Secretary in person has sent us a letter. He does not like the name our township is achieving. Indeed, he is so disturbed by it that he has threatened to go so far as to withdraw the government subsidy for our local police. Well, all I say is – *this!*

He tears the letter and crumples it and grinds it underfoot.

We are a self-governing Socialist community with Dearne and Don and Calder for our inviolate boundaries, and we will continue to press for the resignation of Feng!

HOPEFAST. Barney, did you hear that they've arrested Charlie?

BOOCOCK. Indeed, I did hear it. Why else have I done this?

(He points to the remains of the letter.)

MRS BOOCOCK. Our party cannot afford to be associated with thieves.

BOOCOCK. Sarah!

MRS BOOCOCK. Action has been taken, Barney. Tell him.

HOPEFAST. The natural suspicion attaching to a criminal charge has rendered inexpedient the retention of Alderman Butterthwaite on various committees. Of course, we don't rule out the eventual possibility of rehabilitation.

BOOCOCK. You . . . you can't just vote him out! There aren't sufficient present.

HOPEFAST. Provisionally we can do. The rest can be arranged.

MRS BOOCOCK. It will be arranged. I'm off to see to it now.

Barney, my dear, as usual, you have arrived a bit too tardy. (*She goes out.*)

HARDNUTT. This is a party issue, Barney. You can't stand independent. (*He goes out.*)

HICKLETON. None of us wanted it. None of us like it. (*He goes out.*)

HOPEFAST. Bear in mind, Barney, he *was* short of money. (*He goes out.*)

BOOCOCK (*stamping with frustration*). His Worship the Mayor. His Honour and His Worship. His Grace and His Majesty and His Worship the Mayor . . . Oh, oh, my leg . . .

> *He staggers and falls, knocking the screen over.* BUTTER-THWAITE *is standing at the bar. He is much as in the police station, but wearing a ragged old muffler, and a woollen tam o'shanter over his bandage.*

BUTTERTHWAITE. Aye aye, me old Barney. I heard what was said.

BOOCOCK. Charlie! You're out of jail! They couldn't pin nowt on you! Thank God for that! I believe in you, Charlie. I'm going to combat this sordid betrayal. I will not permit . . .

BUTTERTHWAITE. You can't prevent. The wheel of years is now rotating. I'm voted out. This afternoon, I'm drinking.

BOOCOCK. *I'll* show you my loyalty.

> BUTTERTHWAITE *laughs and* BOOCOCK *goes out.*

BUTTERTHWAITE. Who's drinking with me? Why, is there nobody?

A DRINKER. You gave us the appearance of wanting to be on your own.

BUTTERTHWAITE. Appearances are deceptive. Frank, here you are! You can serve us i' t'back. (*He throws a handful of money on the bar.*) I don't want to see anybody bahn off to their dinners until this is drunk up. But afore you make your

choices, which gentlemen present take an interest in fine
arts?

General giggles.

A DRINKER. If you mean dirty postcards . . .

BUTTERTHWAITE. Not precisely dirty postcards . . . This
good brass I am expending here is the last of all my petty
savings – the dregs of a lifetime of service to the community.
Look, here's me Post Office book – 'Account Closed', do you
see it? . . . Community? What's community? *You?* 'Oh
no,' you said, 'not me,' you said – and rightly said, by Judas –
'leave it to the mugs,' you said, *'we're* lousy.' Well, Charlie's
lousy too: and Charlie bears in mind that the first day of May
is not only a day of Socialist congratulation but also a day of
traditional debauchment in the base of a blossoming hedge-
row . . . *I* pay for the drink, *you* sup it up, and in return
you're going to do what I request – least-roads, I *hope* you
are, for any lad as tries to finkle *me*, by gor, I'll finkle *him* till
his eyes are looking out through the cleft of his armpit . . .
Come on into t'back bar; I'm not calling you twice . . . (*He
leads them all into the inner room.*)

SCENE FOUR

Inside the Copacabana Club . . . now an art gallery.

*Artistic screens hung with paintings occupy the upper part of the
stage. The front stage area is a sort of foyer laid out for a recep-
tion. One table covered with green baize holds catalogues, etc.
Another table set out as a buffet with champagne and sandwiches.
Paperchains from the roof. A white ribbon tied across the back of
the foyer, as a formal barrier preventing access to the pictures.*

GLORIA (*in a very demure dress*) *superintending buffet and
catalogues,* LADY SWEETMAN *and* YOUNG SWEETMAN *hurrying about making last-minute alterations.*

Enter BLOMAX (*he is not noticed by the others on the stage*).

BLOMAX (*to the audience*).

And so we lead on, to the final cruel conclusion
Compounded of corruption and unresolved confusion.
I think the time has come to resolve it, if I can.
Here I stand alone, an embrangled English man
Nerving myself up in the torment of my duty.
The first day of May is the day of Art and Beauty,
The dust of Sweetman thrust into the eye-balls of you all
For to wash you white and whiter than the whitewash on the
    wall.
But out in the dark back lane
The great grey cat still waits by the mouse's hole.
You'll observe the general sense of bygones being bygones
. . . (*He points to* GLORIA.) Who'd recognize her now, stood
ready to draw out the corks for the nobility and gentry? Who
indeed would recognize the premises themselves, where the
only indication of what's under the underwear is on a canvas
by Titian . . . or at least William Etty? Titillation, if you
like, but in a form that even Lady Sweetman regards as
desirable.

> *The room begins to fill.*
>
> SWEETMAN *with wife and son.* FENG, WELLESLEY,
> CONSERVATIVE LADIES, F. J., BOOCOCK, COUNCIL-
> LORS *are present.*
>
> BOOCOCK *wears his chain, but no robes.*

SWEETMAN. Ha-h'm. The opening of a new art gallery is, or
should be, a pleasurable labour, for the benefit of thousands.
Therefore, I will not remind you that works of art – no less
magnificent than those from my collection which already
hang here – are lying at this moment in the cellars of the
Municipal Hospital, unthought-of and unenjoyed . . . but
not, may I hope, for ever? It gives me enormous pleasure to

detect one sign of reconciliation – His Worship the Mayor is with us today, and also many of his . . .

BOOCOCK. Not to be construed as an official occasion but purely as a social courtesy in recognition of cultural attainment.

MRS BOOCOCK. Sir Harold Sweetman, Lady Sweetman, ladies and gentlemen, we feel in the Labour Party that the provision of an art gallery, albeit a worthy objective, does not warrant the expenditure of public money upon what is, after all, a luxury amenity. So all the more do we of the Labour Party welcome the initiative of private enterprise upon this issue. I would like to say . . . 'thank you', Sir Harold. And thank you also, Lady Sweetman; you have done us all a proud and worthy service.

Applause.

SWEETMAN. Yes. Madam Mayoress, thank *you*. Now it only remains that I request my dear wife to formally inaugurate the Gallery.

LADY SWEETMAN. Let me tell you first about the dedication of this Gallery. It is called the 'Sweetman Memorial Gallery', not in memory of Sir Harold, who is still very much with us . . .

BLOMAX *picks up a glass of champagne.*

GLORIA. Hey . . .

BLOMAX. Morituro te salutant!

GLORIA. You get out of here at once!

BLOMAX. No. Dulce et decorum est pro filia pulcherrima incarceri in vinculis. Wellesley, let go of me; you'll undermine me resolution.

LADY SWEETMAN (*trying to ignore his interruption*). . . . but in memory of his father, the late Mr. Fortunatus Sweetman, whose enterprise and industry brought wealth and fortune to us all . . .

BLOMAX. I want to talk to Colonel Feng!

FENG (*to* SWEETMAN). Had you invited Mr Blomax here, sir?

SWEETMAN. Indeed I had not. Are you aware, Doctor, that this is a private function?

BLOMAX. Colonel Feng, observe my daughter. She requires a new father, and behold, here he is! I am washing myself in public with the detergent of self-sacrifice. Five hundred pounds. Take it, Mr Mayor. You know where it comes from.

(*He hands the money to* BOOCOCK.)

BOOCOCK. We all thought you'd been exonerated.

BLOMAX. No, no. I am confessing. And the extraordinary thing is, I had already confessed. I offered Queen's evidence! Why was it refused?

SWEETMAN. Was it, Colonel? Why?

FENG. Queen's evidence, albeit dramatic, is not necessarily sufficient. Or even true. You surely know that, sir.

LADY SWEETMAN (*in desperation*). So it gives me great pleasure to declare the 'Sweetman Memorial Art Gallery' open for all time to the people of this town.

She takes a little pair of scissors and cuts the tape.
Applause.

Now I hope you will all enjoy yourselves and don't go home till you've seen everything.

She and her husband contrive to move the guests up among the pictures. BLOMAX, BOOCOCK *and* FENG *remain in the foyer.* SWEETMAN *returns to them.*

BLOMAX. In any case, I can tell you, my Queen's evidence was highly sufficient – and every word of it was true. I am very sorely afraid I have been deliberately victimized. So I am making my appeal to the high society of the town.

BOOCOCK. This is very very shocking indeed, Wellington. But, Colonel Feng, Dr Blomax has been my medical adviser for a great many years. I think it would show a more humane spirit if you accepted his plea. After all, he *has* returned the money.

SWEETMAN. Yes, Colonel, surely we don't need to press this matter now in regard to Dr Blomax? That is, if he *can* give us all the full details of everything that happened . . .

YOUNG SWEETMAN. That's the voice of two magistrates, Colonel. You can't entirely neglect it.

SWEETMAN. Speak when you're spoken to.

FENG. The decision is *mine*. It is nobody else's. This man is an accomplice, but the thief himself is still at large: and until he is apprehended you must permit me to handle it as best I know how.

WELLESLEY. And handle it inevitably so that my father goes to jail? And he going to jail will leave your conscience clear enough for you to marry me.

BLOMAX. Marry? Him? You? . . . But what about Maurice? I confessed because of *him*!

WELLESLEY. And Colonel Feng confessed. He confessed he was in love with me. So I naturally asked him to destroy his integrity and make it easier for you.

FENG. Naturally.

WELLESLEY. And equally naturally he has been unable to do it. I have often dreamed I would be the beautiful destruction of the strength of a good man. It has turned out to be more comfortable to deal only with feeble ones. What about you, Maurice, how are you for integrity?

YOUNG SWEETMAN. *Me?*

WELLESLEY. Don't worry, I will marry you: because I don't have to respect you and I don't have to continually involve myself in the curls and contortions of an extraordinary code of ethics. Have you even seen a boa-constrictor that strangled itself with itself? . . . Oh dear, I feel so miserable.

The GUESTS *have drifted away from the pictures and the last few speeches have been heard by everyone.*

SWEETMAN. Colonel Feng, is this true? I mean, *have* you proposed to her?

FENG. Yes, sir, it is true, as a matter of observable fact. I will not humiliate myself, Sir Harold, by explaining my motives. But I take it that as a gentleman you will not dispute my word when I inform you most solemnly that my professional integrity has in no whit been compromised by whatever mis-construction this young woman puts upon it, *deliberately* puts upon it. She has *not* destroyed me, no . . . She does not influence me, sir, in one way or the other; my private life is private . . . It appears I am confounded, sir, by endeavour-ing to preserve it so, but . . .

SWEETMAN. But in fact you're telling me that if it wasn't for this little half-dago doxy that bloody robber Butterthwaite would have been behind bars a week since!

F. J. Precisely what side do you imagine you're on!

FENG. Side, do you say, sir, side! I am not, sir, aware of it. I am aware that my *own* side, my private side, Sir Harold, may well indeed be for derision, humiliated and confounded, but, sir, I am not destroyed, sir . . . I am not yet aware of *side !*

BLOMAX. In that case, Colonel Feng, you're the only man present that isn't!

FENG. You! You are not to speak further. I cannot bear it further!

BLOMAX. *I've* had to bear more than *you've* had to bear! I've had to commit myself, and as a result without intention I have dropped my poor friend Charlie where I cannot believe he will ever get out of. I thought when I determined to return the five hundred we could call it a closed book . . . but I see that we can't. Alas, the British police, with their well-known impartiality and their zeal for adamantine truth and justice, are clearly going to triumph yet again. So I now have no choice but to deliver my second preparation – all typed out in quadruplicate. (*He produces some sheets of typescript.*) Oh, Gloria, I beg your pardon, for you this is catastrophe, I have stripped us all fair frozen, with not one obligation left honoured.

He distributes his papers.

Mr Mayor, here's your copy – Chief Constable, yours! Sir Harold, here's yours! The unexpurgated history, gentlemen, of the Copacabana Club that was and Superintendent Wiper that still is, with all his little relationships that even Charlie didn't find out. And by and large the entire question of the bracing and the strutting of your backbone, Colonel Feng!

SWEETMAN (*throwing his paper on the floor*). You will not of course, Colonel, attach any credence to . . .

BOOCOCK. Colonel Feng, you are holding that piece of paper upside down. Permit me to . . .

FENG turns his back and walks away among the pictures. Enter WIPER in a hurry.

WIPER. Where's the Chief Constable? . . . Hello, what's going on?

BLOMAX gives WIPER the fourth copy.

BLOMAX. Mr Mayor, do *you* believe what I've written down on these?

BOOCOCK. I must say I am afraid it is only too plausible . . . Go on, read it, Superintendent. We would like to hear your comments!

WIPER. You jerked-up Jack-in-office, do you not realize what's happening! My comments can wait. I've got a job to do! Sir Harold, I must ask you to close down your gallery.

SWEETMAN. What . . . whatever for?

WIPER. A matter of public order. A quarter of an hour ago Alderman Butterthwaite removed himself from the Victoria

and Albert with the entire mid-morning congregation of that
celebrated resort, and at this present moment he is on his
way out here . . . with half a hundred others, of the lowest
type in town, layabouts, tearaways, every man of 'em half-
seas over!

LADY SWEETMAN. But what does he want!

WIPER. I think he wants to wreck your gallery. We've only just
found out, but it appears he's been working this up for over
a week.

SWEETMAN. Why haven't you stopped him?

WIPER. In the middle of the town? How much open scandal
do you really want to have? Up here we can contain them –
I've given orders for a cordon, but . . .

SWEETMAN. Chief Constable!

F. J. Where is he?

FENG *comes back into the main stage.*

SWEETMAN. Chief Constable, come here. I am holding you
responsible if there is violence or damage, entirely responsible!

FENG.

Violence, damage . . . done already, done,
All violence perpetrated, broken down
In violence, brickwork cracked and fallen, damage,
Responsibility . . . whose? Not long ago
In this elected Council there was in violence
Raised a violent demand I should resign.
I did not notice it. I said that I
Derived authority for my high office not
From the jerk and whirl of irrelevant faction –
You, sir, and you, your democratic Punch and Judy –
But from the Law, being abstract, extant, placed,
Proclaimed 'I am'! But, as you say, sir, now,
Violence and damage, I *do* resign, sir, now.
Good day to you, Superintendent. Law and Order?

Here is your confidence, your credence, *here*
Is your impartial service. *I* resign,
Continue, Mr Wiper . . . Preserve the peace.

*While he is speaking there is a growing clamour outside which
resolves itself into shouts of 'three times three for Charlie B',
etc. . . . and a ragged singing of 'Ilkley Moor'.*
Enter LUMBER *in a hurry, and several* PCs.

LUMBER. Colonel Feng, sir . . .
FENG (*waves him towards* WIPER). No, no, to *him* . . .

FENG *goes upstairs.*

LUMBER (*looking from one to the other*). Er . . . sir?
WIPER. Well?
LUMBER. It's not going too well; we were took by surprise
across the lunch hour; you see, they've all piled on the buses
. . . I'm afraid they'll be in here before I can get a full
cordon. I've three radio cars up already, but one of the lorries
has developed magneto trouble . . . I've ordered out the
mounted squad . . . what about the dogs?

The noise grows.

They're forcing the cordon now! It's sheer weight of numbers! I've got all the PCs lined up on the steps but . . .
WIPER. Get these men to the doors! You, you, you, you –
there, there, there, there!

The PCs *rush off, at his direction, down the aisles to hold the
auditorium doors, which are being forced. Sounds of struggle
from the foyers. Some demonstrators break in. They are
carrying bottles, and placards with such slogans as 'All fine
art is a hearty fart', 'Paint me, paint my dog', 'You can't gild
a mucky lily', 'If the people scrawl, put glazed tiles on the
wall', and so on. Some placards have drawings on them of
women's bodies, etc.*

*The P Cs pursue them and succeed, after fighting in the aisles
or on the stage, in chasing or dragging them out. The doors are
finally held, but only by the utmost efforts of the police.
During the commotion* BUTTERTHWAITE *has come in at the
rear of the stage. He sweeps some plates off the buffet and sits
on the table cross-legged. He helps himself to champagne and
a hunk of iced cake.*

BUTTERTHWAITE. If you've got in mind to rax me off this
table, you can have another think. There's more uses nor one
to a bottle o' bubbly, and I'm proficient in 'em all.

He sings.

As it fell out upon a day, rich Dives he made a feast,
And he invited all his friends and gentry of the best,
But Lazarus he sat down and down and down at Dives' door,
Some meat, some drink, brother Dives, he said, bestow unto
the poor!

FENG. Now, Mr Wiper, what's your next move?
WIPER. *I'm* handling this.
FENG. I know. I am highly entertained, sir.
WIPER. Sergeant . . .

LUMBER *makes a move towards* BUTTERTHWAITE, *who
poises his bottle menacingly. A little* DEMONSTRATOR
*breaks through one of the doors, slips past the P Cs trying to
prevent him, and scuttles on to the stage as though for sanc-
tuary. He squats down at* BUTTERTHWAITE'S *feet, and the*
P C *pursuing him gives up indecisively.*
FENG *turns his back and affects interest in the pictures.*

BUTTERTHWAITE. Now then, Brother Boocock, are you holding up all right, are you? With all them prime Sheffield
knifeblades I've inserted in your shoulder bones.
BOOCOCK. I am still in great part vertical. Which is more than
can be said for you, Charlie. I don't know why you've done

this, but your last remaining friends can do nowt for you now. You have pulled your own self down.

BUTTERTHWAITE. Aye. But there's others aside from me have had their hands on t'ropes, though . . . haven't they, me old Wellington?

BLOMAX. Charlie, I've been pulling on all the ropes round here. Not only on yours.

BUTTERTHWAITE. Go on? Who else is done for?

BLOMAX *makes a gesture towards* FENG.

Oh no, not Colonel Feng! You've not got rid of Feng! Not *you* . . . Oh God, *you!* The subsidence of water . . . After all my subtle skirmishes, my cannonadings, my outflankings . . .

BLOMAX. You yourself were outflanked, Charlie. Although you didn't know it, at the crux of the campaign I was fighting for the Prussians. This unhappy Chief Constable was never at war at all.

BUTTERTHWAITE. Oh, but he was, though . . . he was in treaty with Sweetman.

BLOMAX. You've always enjoyed my little bits o' patter, Charlie. But you should never ha' believed 'em.

BUTTERTHWAITE. So that's how it was . . . the beloved physician . . . Colonel, I say Colonel, I'm talking to *you!* I give you no apology. You're a strong-backboned man and you chose of your own free will to do our dirty work. And if it's turned out a sight dirtier than might have been foretold, I am sure that you will find yourself an occupational philosophy, and remain like Barney Boocock in great part still vertical. Oh, oh, oh, I have lived. I have controlled, I have redistributed. The Commonwealth has gained. The tables have been spread. Not with bread and marge, you know, like they used to in the workhouse, but with a summation of largesse demanding for its attendance soup-spoons in their rank, fish-knives and forks, flesh-knives and forks, spoons

for the pudding, gravy and cruet, caper sauce and mayon-
naise . . . and I by my virtue stood the President of the
feast! . . . All right, you've got the belly-ache, and so I've
got to go. But I don't take it kindly. Philosophy be damned.
There's a foul wind blows over t'moor-top on this cold May-
day morning. The peoples of the world are marching and
rejoicing alongside the saluting-bases, but here I've called to
action a detachment of forces that have never heard a bugle!
My army today is a terrible shambles. Look at 'em, fellow
Councillors; you ruled 'em, *I* ruled 'em, and we never knew
who they were! I'll tell you who they were; they drank and
slept and skived and never punched a bloody clock when
clocks was for the asking. We piped to them and they did not
dance, we sang them our songs and they spat into t'gutter.
(*He pats the little* DEMONSTRATOR's *head.*) I was the grand
commander of the whole of my universe. Now all that's left
me is the generalship of these. I need to assume a different
order o' raiment. (*He pulls the baize tablecloth to him and
arranges it like a shawl.*) Three times three, but all that's left
is paper.

He pulls down a paper chain and hangs it round his neck.

Three times three is nine, but the old cocked hat's bashed in.
So here's a replacement.

*He picks up a ring of flowers that has been garnishing the
buffet and puts it on his head.*

. . . In my rejection I have spoken to this people. I will
rejoice despite them. I will divide Dewsbury and mete out
the valley of Bradford; Pudsey is mine, Huddersfield is mine,
Rotherham also is the strength of my head, Osset is my law-
giver, Black Barnsley is my washpot, over Wakefield will I
cast out my shoe, over Halifax will I triumph. Who will bring
me into the strong city, who will lead me into the boundaries

of Leeds ? Wilt not thou, oh my deceitful people, who hast cast me off ? And wilt not thou go forth with Charlie ?

LITTLE DEMONSTRATOR. Hey ey, we're going, we're all going forth together!

BUTTERTHWAITE. No. Oh no. Oh no, you aren't. The only place you're going is into t'black maria.

Police car noises from offstage and voices giving orders.

LUMBER (*to* WIPER). Sir, it's the reinforcements . . .

WIPER. Right, Mr Butterthwaite, we'd like a word with you outside.

The PCs *drag out the* DEMONSTRATOR, *and then come for* BUTTERTHWAITE, *who lets himself go limp. As* BUTTER-THWAITE *is removed up the aisle, he sings:*

BUTTERTHWAITE.

Out he goes the poor old donkey
Out he goes in rain and snow,
For to make the house place whiter
Who will be the next to go ?

Clean the kitchen and the parlour,
Scrub the wall and scrub the floor,
Clean the hoofmarks off the lino
And the smears from off the door.

Climb a ladder and wipe the windows,
Swill the roof with water clear,
Pour your soap suds down the chimney
Till none can tell what beast was here.

When all is washed and all is scoured
And all is garnished bright as paint,
Who will come with his six companions
And a stink to make you faint ?

The song is taken up by those outside the theatre, and con-cludes (if time allows) with a fortissimo reprise of the first stanza.

SWEETMAN. Thank you, Superintendent. Most commendably accomplished, sir.

BOOCOCK. There is still a very great deal to be gone into and sorted out. Nothing of what has happened redounds to any-one's credit. So who's going to make a start and establish a fair inquiry?

BLOMAX. Oh it's not so bad as all that. The start has already been made. Our accumulated garbage has all been carted out and there's nothing more to do now but to polish the sides of the dustbin a bit and keep away the horse-flies. The Con-servative Party, on balance, will find the whole business . . .

SWEETMAN. The whole business should, on balance, weigh slightly to our advantage.

F. J. I think it should.

SWEETMAN. Yes.

BLOMAX. While the Labour Party, on the other hand . . .

HARDNUTT AND HICKLETON. We prefer to defer comment upon this unsavoury episode.

HOPEFAST AND MRS BOOCOCK. But we wish nevertheless to publicly dissociate ourselves from it.

ALL THE COUNCILLORS AND MRS BOOCOCK. We lay the matter with confidence before the good sense of the elec-torate.

BLOMAX. The Superintendent will resign . . .

WIPER. Of my own free will, please note, no questions asked, *and* I get a pension.

BLOMAX. My darling daughter Wellesley will marry her fiancé . . . Go on, go on, give him a kiss.

WELLESLEY *does so.*

And in consideration of my future tact and silence on all

public occasions, I, her useless father, shall be liberally accepted into the bosom of his family. (*He shakes* SWEETMAN *by the hand.*) How d'you do, sir?

SWEETMAN. How d'you do?

BLOMAX. Lady Sweetman . . . ?

LADY SWEETMAN. My dear Doctor . . .

BLOMAX. May I present my dear wife?

LADY SWEETMAN. I would be delighted, Doctor. My dear Mrs Blomax . . .

BLOMAX. It's really so much tidier and altogether less awkward. I have made arrangements for a private maternity ward in Leeds . . .

WIPER. To be, of course, defrayed from the aforementioned pension.

BLOMAX. Wellesley, my darling, why don't you kiss him again? No one's going to interfere.

She does so.

ALL AS CHORUS (*except* FENG).

No one's going to *dare* to interfere.

FENG. I am very sorry, Miss Blomax, to have exposed you to the imperfections of your person at so unseasonable a time. I trust that it will not be long before you regain your equilibrium. Gentlemen, I am going to London. I shall inform the Home Secretary how much I have appreciated the efficiency and speed with which the Superintendent dealt with this . . . Gangway, if you please, I'm coming through . . . (*He leaves.*)

ALL.

We stand all alone to the north of the Trent
You leave us alone and we'll leave you alone
We take no offence where none has been meant
But you hit us with your fist, we'll bash *you* with a stone!
Withdraw those quivering nostrils

We smell as we think decent
If we tell you we've cleaned our armpits
You'd best believe we've cleaned 'em recent.
We have washed them white and whiter
Than the whitewash on the wall
And if for THE WORKHOUSE DONKEY
We should let one tear down fall
Don't think by that he's coming back . . .
The old sod's   gone for good and all!

THE END

ALTERNATIVE SPEECHES FOR PROLOGUE AND EPILOGUE

(1) BLOMAX' *opening speech (Act One):*

Ladies and gentlemen, I am a native
Of the Greater London conurbation.
I found at first your northern parts not very conducive
To what was perhaps my more courtly mode of deportment:
But having arrived here I soon made the adjustment,
Involving geographically an appreciable mutation,
(I mean, in landscape, climate, odours, voices, food).
I put it to you that such a journey needs
In the realm of morality an equal alteration.
I mean, is there anything you really believe to be bad ?
If you lived in the south you might well think it good.
You might well think, as I do,
That you should change the shape of your faces,
Or even double their number
When you travel between two places.
The values of other people
Are not quite as you understand them.
I would not overpraise them,
I would not recommend them,
I am certainly not here in order to condemn them.
From the beginning to the end
Each man is bound to act
According to his nature
And the nature of his land.
Your land is different from theirs.
Why, (county by county*) it has its own music.

*   *   *

(2) *Concluding* CHORUS (*Act Three*):

We stand all alone to the north of the Trent
Let them leave us alone and we'll leave them alone
We take no offence where none has been meant
But they hit us with their fist, we'll bash 'em back with a stone!
They can pull up their damn nostrils,
We smell as we think decent.
If we tell them we've cleaned our armpits
They'd best believe we've cleaned them recent.
We have washed them white and whiter
Than the whitewash on the wall
And if for the WORKHOUSE DONKEY
We should let one tear down fall . . .
Nobody need think that he's going to come back:
The old black leech is gone for good and all!

        *   *   *

   * Words in parenthesis to be omitted in the West Riding of
Yorkshire.

Methuen's Modern Plays
EDITED BY JOHN CULLEN AND GEOFFREY STRACHAN